A PRACTICAL GUIDE TO

ZERO WASTE
for Families

BY FREDRIKA SYREN

A PRACTICAL GUIDE TO

ZERO WASTE
for Families

BY FREDRIKA SYREN

Build. Buzz. Launch.
Media & Publishing
Dallas, TX

Zero Waste for Families - A Practical Guide
Second Edition 2022

Copyright © 2022 The Zero Waste Family®

www.ZeroWasteFamily.com

Published by BBL Publishing, an imprint of
Build.Buzz.Launch. Media & Publishing, Dallas TX, 75218
www.buildbuzzlaunch.com

22 23 24 25 26 / 10 9 8 7 6 5 4 3 2 1
ISBN: 979-8-9854660-0-3 (trade paperback)
ISBN: 978-1-7352966-9-2 (eBook)
Library of Congress Control Number: 2022902920

Book cover and interior design: Kaspar deLine
deLine & Co. Communications and Design

Cover Photograph: Elena Shur Photography

Manufactured in the United States of America

For permission requests, print copies, or author interviews
contact write to the publisher: info@buildbuzzlaunch.com.

Dedication:
This book is dedicated to my three
wonderful children, Isabella, Noah and Liam,
for always being my inspiration.

Contents

Zero waste car kit evelibearum conesti undiae ditisi

Introduction

*"My kids should not have to worry about plastic waste
in the ocean, pesticides in their food or climate change.
They should only have to worry about school, if a boy likes
them, or if I will notice they took an extra cookie."*

— Fredrika Syren

I think most people assume I was "born green."

The truth is that before 2006, while I did favor organic food and I did recycle… that was about it. I knew about climate change and was concerned about it—but it wasn't until I became a mother that I felt a deep sense of urgency. Fueled by that maternal, protective instinct to leave my children with a healthy planet to call home long after I'm gone, we've slowly (and clumsily, at times) embraced a zero-waste lifestyle — and we're figuring it out as we go.

When it comes to climate change, I think many of us tune out simply because we don't know what we can do. But since my family and I started our journey to more sustainable living over a decade ago, I can tell you that it feels good to actually take steps to make a difference, even if they are small. I did not choose to become an activist, but I chose to be active. This was how my journey toward living a more sustainable life began.

As we journeyed towards our zero waste life, I looked for any information — especially how to reduce waste with kids — but found very little was available. Once we achieved our zero waste goal, I wanted to share our tricks and tips with other families looking to become more sustainable, and this became the first edition of this book. Since then, I have been asked about how we talk to our kids about climate change and how we turn fear into action, so I wanted to make a second edition of my book, adding more information about these topics, as well as more recipes I have since created and additional resources.

In 2021, the United Nations' Intergovernmental Panel on Climate Change released a report that declared a "code red for humanity" and gave a grim glimpse of the world's future. The report's statement that climate change is caused by humans may

Zero waste family Urban Homestead

We're a zero waste family of five, and together we fight for a cleaner, healthier planet by speaking up, inspiring, and volunteering to preserve the planet and a future for our three children.

be the most damaging part. With every part of the globe affected by the actions of humans, seeing the alarming outlook could have us asking ourselves: What can I do about climate change? I'm just one person?

The answer? Well, it isn't just recycling.

It's easy to feel overwhelmed with all the negative information and get the feeling you want to just ignore the whole thing. But personal action is critical, and as individuals, we should always do what we can to reduce our own carbon footprint and strive to leave the planet in better shape for future generations

My family and I have been working on this since 2006. Once we made the decision to reduce our carbon footprint, we executed small changes over many years. I truly believe it takes baby steps to go green and that you have to challenge yourself over years because few people can carry out drastic changes right away.

For over 14 years, we have been taking measures toward a more sustainable life. I still feel there is room for improvement, and there are days when I just want to throw in the towel and give up. And then I'm reminded of why I do this — my kids — so they will have a planet to live on and to make sure they grow up as healthy as possible.

When we decided to go completely zero waste in 2015, we were living in an apartment in Sweden. Today we live on an urban homestead located on a standard-sized lot in the middle of San Diego. Together as a family, we care for our 400-square-foot backyard garden , which sources many of our meals. While living zero waste has been challenging and has often required creativity, we always knew the end result would be worth the hard work. I knew that reducing our waste to almost nothing would benefit the planet, but we've been surprised by how our zero waste lifestyle has also saved us lots of money. Now we're on the road to financial independence. Because we save so much money by consuming less and living simply, we have more time with our children and with each other — which has made our family a very happy one. Our lives feel richer, even as we've learned to live with less.

I'm so happy you are here and you have taken the first step in your journey towards a sustainable life. I hope this guide will help you take small steps, because I always recommend you start small, one step at a time, celebrate your accomplishments and remember to enjoy the journey. This is how our family's path began. Today we are a family of five, living a zero-waste, plant-based, & mindfully minimal life so that both our kids and our planet can enjoy a beautiful, thriving future.

We created this guide in hopes of making the shift to zero waste feel less overwhelming. We've collected tips, recipes, life hacks, and brands that have helped us along the way, and we are excited to share them with you.

In this updated guide, I share even more tips, recipes and ideas, and offer helpful information about sustainable products. I have added a couple more chapters about how to practice zero waste gardening, since gardening is a very big part of our zero waste lifestyle. I have also added a chapter about how to talk to kids about climate change and how to raise environmentally friendly kids. We hope you'll join this ever-growing Zero Waste Family that's building a conscious shift towards sustainability — because the truth is, there's no time to waste.

Follow us on social media and join the conversation there as well.

Website www.Zerowastefamily.com
Instagram @thezero.waste.family
Facebook https://www.facebook.com/thezerowastefamily/
YouTube https://www.youtube.com/zerowastefamily

Noah, Liam, Isabella and James Hiking

Chapter 1

Think Big, Start Small

"Think big and start small. First, look at the big picture: by reducing your waste by just 20%, you will make a positive change for the environment. Small changes matter! But you have to start somewhere."

– Fredrika Syren

Are you feeling overwhelmed yet?

I know I was when I first learned about zero waste. The good news is there's plenty we can do — and small-scale changes make a huge difference. Significantly reducing waste is a challenge by itself. But living zero waste while raising children might seem like a nearly impossible task.

A zero waste family lifestyle is not something anyone can achieve overnight because it requires dedication, teamwork, attention, and *it happens over time*. The good news is that it's quite feasible. The best part is that by attempting this as a family, you will influence — if not change — your children's habits, thereby helping them continue this lifestyle once they're on their own someday.

Think big and start small is my suggestion. First, look at the big picture: by reducing your waste just 20%, you will make a positive change for the environment. Small changes matter! But you have to start somewhere.

The initial step toward reducing household waste is paying attention to what you buy – as well as its packaging. See if you can buy the same products package-free in bulk or by bringing your own containers. Go through your garbage at the end of the week to see what really is in there. Set small goals first. Then, over time, work toward larger ones.

Here's how we started small

1. We removed the trash can.

My husband was smart and decided to simply move our kitchen trash can to

Fredrika and Isabella with chickens, Amelia and Gunilla. The chickens are a great part of how we reduce waste – they eat our compost and provide fertilizer for the garden.

the hallway closet. This way, we really had no excuses — we had no choice but to look at everything we needed to discard and see if it could be composted, reused, or recycled somehow. When we did have trash, we had to walk down the hall to throw it away — which gave us a moment to think about how we could stop bringing those items into the house in the first place.

2. We reduced what we bought.

We now really have to think about how we can avoid buying or accepting anything that will result in waste. For example, we try very hard not to buy anything packaged. Our philosophy is simple: if we can't reuse, recycle, or rot it — we won't buy it.

3. We started buying in bulk.

We try to buy in bulk whenever possible, avoid fruits and veggies with stickers, and avoid processed foods altogether. We switched from plastic toothbrushes to compostable, biodegradable, bamboo ones. We make our own dishwasher soap, cleaning supplies, and beauty products—which is not as hard as it seems.

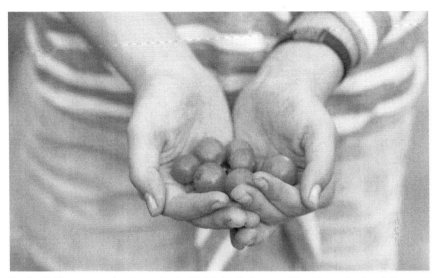

Our family lives on an urban homestead, which is basically a small farm in our backyard. There we grow 70% of all the food our family of five eats.

4. We invested in compost.

Anything that can rot and is vegetarian can go into the compost. So for us, all food scraps, paper clippings, and even our toothbrushes go into the compost. We use a couple of different compost methods: Bokashi, garden compost, and worm compost — and our chickens eat most of our food compost. Composting is great because waste turns into pure nutrients for the planet. Plus, my kids think the little "wigglers" (their endearing name for the worms) are very entertaining—they consider them pets.

5. We did a trash audit.

In order to reduce our waste to very little, we had to know what we were throwing into the trash. This is why a waste audit was necessary. The fact is that we couldn't know where we needed to make changes if we didn't truly understand our actions and consumption. To perform a trash audit, you collect and sort all your waste before putting it out for collection. You look through what you have collected and try to identify patterns, areas for improvement, and look for waste-free replacements for items.

The 5R's of Zero Waste

As you're beginning your zero waste adventure, keep it simple with the mantra of the "5 Rs": *Refuse, Reduce, Reuse, Rot, and Recycle.*

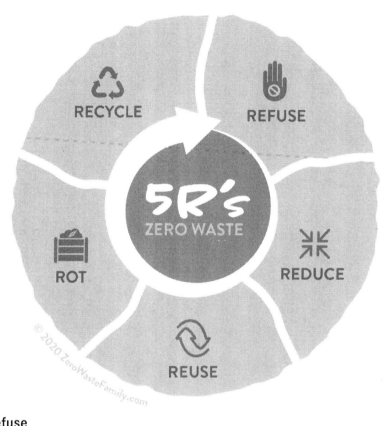

Refuse

Just say no to what you do not need, like single-use disposable bags, straws, cutlery, and cups. It only takes a few minutes to "unsubscribe" from junk mail and promotional freebies which might as well be a one-way ticket to the garbage bin.

Reduce

Reduce what you need by shopping with a purpose — focusing on necessary purchases rather than random splurges. Too often these "extra" items (fast fashion, cheap electronic gadgets, processed foods) make their way into the dumpster, back of the closet, or come wrapped in unsustainable packaging.

Reuse

Invest in reusable items you use often. Switch out disposable items for reusable and permanent alternatives. This means sourcing a reusable beverage container and carrying it with you when you are out and about. It means carrying reusable cutlery with you in an effort to avoid disposable cutlery. Invest in a refillable glass or stainless steel water bottle to part ways with plastic bottles for good! And arm yourself with an assortment of reusable fabric bags for your produce and other unpackaged foods.

Rot

Composting all organic matter is a very easy way to reduce waste and turn it into fertilizer that's crucial for healthy soil.

Recycle

Recycle what you can't reduce or reuse to keep it out of the landfill.

I honestly thought that going zero waste would be more work. I guess in some ways it is, but my husband and I agree that a little extra work is worth it. We also don't have to argue about who takes out the trash anymore! The best part is that our kids are completely engaged and act as though we never even had a trash can in the first place. Instead, they make a sport out of discovering what they can build with materials they find in our recycling bin.

Fun Fact

For the average household, 20% of their household trash is food scraps and waste. If you can divert that food into a compost to enrich our soils, you are already on the road to Zero Waste!

Chapter 2

Shopping Zero Waste

"Unless someone like you cares a whole awful lot, nothing is going to get better. It's not."

— **Dr Seuss**, The Lorax

The easiest way to reduce waste when grocery shopping is to invest in some good-quality reusable shopping bags, produce bags, and large jars with lids.

In my experience, you can never have enough shopping and produce bags because inevitably they get lost, dirty, or lent out to friends. To solve this mystery of the disappearing bags, I always keep a bundle of them in the car. We also love shopping at our local farmers market where reusable bags are encouraged and we can buy in bulk. We have a local co-op that sells lots of organic, local, and bulk foods at a very reasonable price. We usually shop there every other week and at the farmers market every week.

Bulk shopping is a great way to shop zero waste because it eliminates packaging and reduces the carbon footprint. Less packaging means less trash ends up in the landfill.

Bulk Shopping

One essential part of going zero waste is buying in bulk as much as possible. Today I buy almost everything in bulk: flour, grains, nuts, beans, shampoo, conditioner, spices, oils, chocolate, coffee, hemp seeds, dried fruits, snacks, maple syrup, and of course — fruits and vegetables.

So I can easily see what's in each jar, I like to store my bulk foods in glass. That way, the food stays fresh and safe from pests such as kitchen moths, and I can see how much of everything I have left. Buying in bulk cuts down on product packaging, transportation costs, reduces waste, and is usually cheaper — both cost-effective and good for the environment.

Too much of all food packaging is unnecessary and could be prevented because it exists purely for marketing purposes. According to repsly.com, food packaging accounts for about 8-10 percent of food's cost. A study by Portland University found that companies marketing bulk foods versus packaged foods would see an average 54% reduction in material and delivery costs on items including bulk confections, dried fruit, nuts, and trail mix.

Bulk foods require minimal packaging. Naturally, if you buy your bulk in plastic bags, that creates more waste. Instead, do what we do: simply bring the glass jars with you and fill them directly. When you get to the store, weigh each jar and write the weight on a sticker. You don't even need to fully empty your jars — just update the weight, fill it, and pay.

When grocery shopping, we bring our own containers for bulk shopping and reusable cloth produce bags for vegetables and fruits.

Farmers Market

A Farmers Market is a great place to shop package-free and in bulk. Usually, vendors there will happily let you bring your own produce bags and shopping bags.

We try to shop at local farmers markets for as much of our food as possible. We're lucky to have one relatively close to our home. Our family has learned to eat according to the seasons, but we never feel deprived of anything or think we're eating the same thing over and over again. Seriously, besides local and seasonal fruits, veggies, and nuts, you can find eggs, milk, cheese, fish and sea foods, bread, other baked goods, chocolate, mushrooms, meat, poultry and honey. I guess what some feel they can't find, depending on the season, is the variety of fruits or vegetables they normally would buy at a grocery store. But items not in season have traveled long distances, sometimes even from another country. Compared to buying imported goods, buying local avoids more fuel use and CO_2 emissions.

Our local farmers market is on Saturdays. We go as a family and everyone enjoys it. There is something special about smelling and tasting all these wonderful goodies. I also love talking to the vendors and getting to know the people who grow my food.

Buying locally has a positive impact on the environment because there's significantly less energy used and less pollution of the environment involved in the production, distribution and sale of any particular item.

In the food you purchase at an organic farmers market, there are minimal or no preservatives, chemicals, pesticides, herbicides, or synthetic fertilizers. Furthermore, when buying your produce locally, you're doing more than making a healthy choice: you're supporting sustainable and local agricultural practices, which in turn helps to save the earth. You are supporting the local economy and small organic businesses instead of large corporations or GMO foods.

Spending money at the farmers markets is making a big impact. A report published by USDA announced that the number of farmers markets has grown significantly in the last decade. In 2011, one thousand new markets opened. Farmers markets grew from 1,755 in 1994 to 8,144 in 2013 in the U.S alone.

When we spend our money at farmers markets, not only will the demand for more markets increase, but there will also be greater demand for more organic and humane farms. As a result, this could create tens of thousands of jobs. I encourage everyone to pick up your baskets or cloth shopping bags and head to a local farmers market, taste some delicious ripe food, and learn more about your local food.

Watch Out for Greenwashing!

Ever since we've committed to using only eco-friendly products, I have marveled at the way consumers' high demand for greener choices has created a world of trendy options. As a consumer, it's easy to get swept up in the hype and believe all the advertisements, when in reality there's this sneaky little technique called "greenwashing" to watch for… not all products are equal. The cold hard truth is that some are not as environmentally friendly or advantageous as they claim to be.

So, what exactly is "greenwashing"? The term refers to a company or group's misleading advertising of its products as both good for the planet and consumers. Products promoted this way include personal care items, household cleaners, and many disposable commodities. While the green way has created a huge market for green products — in the end, the main goal of all companies is to make a profit. At best, greenwashing is a marketing ploy that also unfortunately hurts the environment. So, a consumer fooled by the greenwashing technique might think they are doing something great when, in fact, it's exactly the opposite.

Here's how to avoid being greenwashed

1. Read labels

Reading labels is so important when it comes to food and other products like cleaning and personal hygiene merchandise. I always say, *the shorter the list, the better—and if you can't pronounce it, don't buy it*. If there is a new food item available, I will google any ingredient I'm unfamiliar with because I can learn a lot quickly— what the ingredients are, or if there are any problems with them, for instance.

2. **Learn about misleading words**

"Natural" can mean a whole lot of things, and usually products are not as "natural" as we might think. "Free-range" can mean that even though chickens are not cramped in a small cage, they might still be trapped inside and living in inhumane conditions. Another word to watch out for is "compostable." Just because a cup is compostable plastic does not mean it will decompose if you send it to a landfill.

3. **Learn about product certifications**

Find some truly sustainable companies and know their certification logos, for example, certified organic, fair trade and non-GMO.

4. **Don't be fooled by the images**

Sure, the package is the color of nature and the baby looks happy — but are those diapers truly eco-friendly? What is it that makes them so? It sounds great that an oil company is helping clean up wildlife trapped in an oil spill — but how green is their practice, really? Look beyond the image and learn more before buying the product.

Facts about Plastic

Only 9% of plastic is actually recycled.

Because we put plastic in the recycling bin, along with paper, cardboard and glass, it seems like it must be recycled at the same rates. That's simply not true! Over 90% of plastic isn't (and often can't be) recycled and ends up in our landfill.

- Every piece of plastic ever produced is still on our planet... 18.2 trillion pounds!
- Within 30 years, plastic in our oceans will outweigh fish.
- The average person inadvertently consumes a credit card's weight of plastic every week!
- Plastic is made from oil. Plastic pollutes our planet from extraction to manufacturing to use and disposal.

Chapter 3

Cleaning Without Waste Or Chemicals

"Going back to a simpler life is not a step backwards."

— **Yvon Chouinard**, *Founder of Patagonia, Inc.*

A side from the packaging, traditional store-bought household cleaners contain chemicals that linger in the air we breathe. They are not safe for children, pets, or any of us because they enter our bodies by absorption through the skin or ingestion of household dust and chemical residues left on dishes and cutlery. After we've finished cleaning and these chemicals are flushed down the drain, they then cause great damage to the environment, oceans, and wildlife.

By making our own household cleaners, we can reduce waste through eliminating packaging — and save money, too. Most importantly, homemade cleaners contain no chemicals harmful to your family or the planet. Since we've switched from store-bought to homemade cleaners, I have noticed that my kids are very sensitive to the smell of chemicals or perfumes and can detect any hint of harmful elements.

Oven Cleaner

¼ cup of dish soap
½ cup baking soda
½ cup coarse sea salt
warm water

Make a paste with the soap, baking powder, and salt. Using a gloved hand, cover the oven with the paste and let it sit overnight. With a damp sponge, using the scrubby as needed, wipe out the oven. Give it a final rinse with warm water.

Thieves Oil *All-Purpose Spray*

32 oz spray bottle
2 cup water
½ cup distilled white vinegar
1 tsp pure Castile soap
¾ cup hydrogen peroxide
20 drops Thieves oil

Fill the bottle with water. Add vinegar,
Castile soap, hydrogen peroxide, Thieves Oil.

Common household items to use for cleaning

Baking soda Great as an all-purpose scrubber, grout cleaner, oven cleaner and sink cleaner, or for removing grease.

Lemon Use for scrubbing sinks, cleaning the fridge and cutting boards, and de-griming glass coffee pots.

Borax Cleans grout and mildew. Effective for removing pencil and crayon marks.

Soap Unscented liquid soap without petroleum distillates (such as Dr. Bronner's - Sal Suds) cleans almost everything.

Cornstarch Shampoos, carpets, and rugs.

Vinegar Cuts grease and cleans mildew.

Tea tree, Thieves, lemon, and lavender essential oils Tea tree and Thieves oils are naturally antiseptic, anti-fungal, and disinfectant. Lavender and lemon are gentle antiseptics and antibacterial, too.

Household Cleaning Recipes:

Here are some recipes I use for making my own household cleaners. These formulas are effective and guaranteed to save you money:

Scrub for tubs, showers, and sinks Baking soda + lemon juice

Window and mirror cleaner Vinegar + newspaper

Toilet bombs

1 cup baking soda
¼ cup citric acid
2 tbsp dish soap
4 drops of tee tree essential oil
silicon ice cube tray

Blend all 4 ingredients in a large bowl and mix well with a whisk. Press mixture into silicon molds and remove any excess mix around the mold. Dry overnight. Remove from molds and keep in airtight container. To clean the toilet, place one bomb in toilet and it will begin to sizzle. Clean with a toilet brush and Viola! Your toilet should be clean.

Soft Cleaning Scrub for sinks and bathtubs

1 cup of baking soda
2 tbsp Castile soap
15 drops of Thieves essential oil
¼ cup of water

Combine baking soda, castile soap and essential oils. Add enough water to make a smooth liquid paste, then transfer mixture to an airtight container.

DIY Scented Cleaning Vinegar

Orange-scented vinegar will cut through grease and help remove any stains. For this, you will require just one cup of orange peelings per jar.

Lemon-scented vinegar you also need one cup of lemon peelings. This recipe becomes a great disinfectant that is especially good for bathroom tiles, sinks and toilet bowls.

Rosemary-scented vinegar includes an antibacterial that is good for wiping tabletops and counter spaces. To create the rosemary scent, add 4 to 8 sprigs of fresh rosemary.

Pine Scented Vinegar works its magic on wood surfaces, including cutting boards. A few clippings from a nearby pine tree will suffice.

You can also substitute citrus peels and herbs with 20 drops of essential oils.

Instructions

- Deposit either fruit peelings or herb sprigs into a large Mason jar or glass jar of any size.
- Add distilled white vinegar to fill the jar almost to the top. Seal with a lid.
- Let the mixture sit for 12 to 24 hours.
- Pour the scented vinegar into a spray dispenser with some peelings or herbs.
- You can add a few squirts in the washing machine as a softener.

Chapter 4
Cooking
Without Waste

"Cooking from scratch is one of the best things you can do for your family's health, your pocketbook, and the planet.

– Fredrika Syren

One way to reduce waste and live a zero waste lifestyle is to cook at home from scratch. When I tell people I do this, I typically get lots of questions about how I have the time and energy to do that. I wish people knew me: I consider myself lazy, and I like to have things done quickly — especially when I have three hungry children standing next to me. Cooking with three hungry kids can sometimes feel like competing on the TV show "Chopped "— I have a few random ingredients, limited time, and some of the harshest food critics critiquing the final meal.

In general, processed and takeout foods come with lots of waste: from stickers to petroleum-based plastic wrap, Styrofoam and aluminum trays, cans to preserve them, and rubber bands to hold it all together. Most of these things cannot be recycled. Besides the waste, the foods packaged in these materials also can expose us to Bisphenol A or BPA— so breaking free from processed and takeout food serves both the environment and our own health.

How do we start cooking from scratch, then? First of all, if you aren't a fan of cooking, then try learning just a few simple recipes. My family's favorite dishes are some of the easiest ones: creamy broccoli soup, bean tacos, lentil stew, and pasta with tomato sauce (find the recipes at ZeroWasteFamily.com). As a mom, I have learned over the years that children really do favor simple foods. When I'm under time constraints, I make bowls with rice, quinoa or potatoes, beans, lettuce, and some sauce or salsa.

I like to store my bulk foods in glass so we can easily see what is in each jar and what needs to be added to the grocery list. Glass also keeps the food fresh and safe from pests such as kitchen moths.

Reducing food waste is key for reducing both food bills and waste in general, so my tip is to come up with creative recipes using the food you have at home. Since I'm cooking for a family of five, I have made my life a lot easier by creating a meal plan that includes very simple recipes — and I stick to it because planning things ahead saves me time and money. Our meals are mostly vegan, but even if you eat meat, it is still possible to cook from scratch without spending the entire day at the stove (even chicken or fish do not take that long to cook).

A great way to save energy and time is by multitasking. For example, while the casserole is in the oven, roast veggies simultaneously. I love crockpots and constantly use mine to save time. I prepare food in the morning in order to have a healthy and delicious meal ready to eat by evening. The following recipe is simple, but yummy.

Using Your Food Scraps

Making your own stock is super easy, and a great way to reduce waste and save some money at the same time. Since I'm vegan, I make vegetable stock, but stock can be made from fish bones and chicken carcasses as well. I make my stock from kitchen scraps so, basically, I save any peels and stems, and tops from onions, garlic, root vegetables, herbs, and so on. I might even add any vegetables that are getting a bit soft. Whenever I cook, I save any scraps in a Mason jar in the freezer. When it's full or I'm out of stock, I then make my stock. This is a fantastic way to use what otherwise

Lentil and tomato stew

1   8 oz can tomato sauce
1   cup red lentils, rinsed
1   large potato, peeled and diced
1   cup mushrooms, sliced
1   cup leafy greens such as spinach, kale, beet tops, swiss chard, minced
2   cup vegetable stock
¼   cup tomato paste
1   tbsp agave nectar
1   tbsp dried oregano
1   tsp smoked paprika

Put everything except the nutritional yeast in a crockpot and cook on high for 4 hours or on low for 8 hours. Before serving, add nutritional yeast and stir.

would become garbage. I tend not to use beet peels or beet greens because they will turn stock red. And I don't use kale stems because they might make the stock bitter. The leftover vegetables after cooking the stock can be composted (or fed to chickens, in my case), but you can make a wonderfully flavorful vegetable salt, also.

Save Money, Reduce Food Waste

Save money and reduce food waste by using every single part of the fruits, veggies, and some of the other foods you buy — including parts normally thrown away! Unfortunately, because we have a tendency to forget what is in our fridge or freezer, it can become food waste. And food waste accounts for half of all waste in landfills. To avoid this, here are my tricks for cooking with food scraps that otherwise would be squandered.

Beet Greens

Most people throw away beet greens, a very underappreciated part of the vegetable. They are as highly nutritious as kale, even more so than the beet bulb itself, and contain high amounts of antioxidants and other phytonutrients. Beet greens and stems are very tasty and mild. I like to eat them braised in olive oil with garlic and shallots, a dash of balsamic vinegar, and salt and pepper. Braise them covered for 4–6 minutes, until tender.

Scrap Vegetable Stock

8   cups water
2-3 cups of vegetable scraps
2   bay leaves
a few sprigs of parsley and thyme,
    (*optional*)
2   pinches of salt
1   piece of kombu seaweed (*optional*
    but adds a nice flavor)

In a large stockpot, add all ingredients. Bring to a boil, then reduce to a simmer for about 1 hour. Strain stock by pouring it through a fine mesh strainer into a large heat-proof bowl or pot. Put solids aside. Once it's completely cool, transfer stock to mason jars or freeze it in smaller portions like ice cube trays.

Stale Bread

I would think that stale bread is one of the most commonly wasted foods because, let's face it, who likes stale bread? Not me. Before going zero waste, I threw out lots of bread. But these days, I employ creative methods to use up every slice. Stale bread can be used to make croutons, to make panzanella salad, to make bread crumbs, bread pudding, or French toast.

Veggie Scrap Broth

Making broth is super easy, and can be used for soups and stews. I always use leftover veggie scraps for it. I simply freeze any garlic and onion ends, peels, etc., until I have collected enough for a batch. See above for the recipe.

DIY Apple Cider Vinegar

1. Clean the jar thoroughly with soap and hot water and let air dry.
2. Fill the jar ¾ full with apple scraps. If you are using whole apples, roughly chop them.
3. Dissolve 2 TBSP cane sugar into 2 cups of water for a quart-sized jar. (Double this for the half-gallon size.) Mix enough to completely cover the apples.
4. Pour sugar water over apples until completely submerged.
5. Weigh down apples with a sterilized fermentation weight or smaller glass jar. Any apples that are exposed to air could mold.
6. Cover jar with cheesecloth or coffee filter, and secure with a rubber band or canning lid.
7. Store in a dark place with consistent room temperature.
8. Let sit for approximately 3 weeks. Check every few days to make sure the apples are staying submerged and no mold is growing.
8. After 3 weeks, strain out the apple pieces and return the liquid to the jar. (The scraps will still be suitable for the compost pile.)
10. Cover the jar with cheesecloth or coffee filter as before, and return to a dark spot for another 3-4 weeks, stirring every few days.
11. At some point during fermentation, you will probably notice a SCOBY that forms on the top. This is the "mother." Just leave it floating in the vinegar.
12. When the apple cider vinegar has reached your desired level of "tartness" you can seal it with a proper lid and start using it!

Apple Scrap Vinegar

Don't waste apple cores and peels. I always like using peels and the cores to make apple cider vinegar. You can make apple cider vinegar from the whole apple, so don't worry if you don't have leftover peels or cores. If you only occasionally use apples, you can store the peels and cores in the freezer until you have gathered enough to start a batch.

Organic apples are always best, especially if you will be using the peel. If you cannot find organic apples, peel them first and discard the peel; use only the inside portion.

A few notes:

- The sugar in the recipe is necessary to "feed" the bacteria but most (if not all) of the sugar is fermented out. Honey does not work well.
- White scum will form on the top. This is normal. Mold, however, will spoil your apple cider vinegar. Be sure that the apples stay submerged in the water. This will help prevent mold. Use a fermentation weight or even a smaller glass jar (thoroughly clean both).
- Gnats and flies love ACV, so you need to make sure your jar is well covered. However, it needs to be able to breathe and release fermentation gasses, so do not use a solid lid. Layers of cheesecloth or a coffee filter work well.

Supplies & Ingredients

- Clean, sterilized jar (wide mouth quart or half gallon pickle)
- Organic apple scraps (enough to fill your jar ¾ full)
- Organic cane sugar
- Filtered water
- Fermentation weight or small glass jar (also sterilized)
- Cheesecloth or coffee filter
- Rubber band or canning lid

Broccoli Stems

Never throw away broccoli stems and leaves because they are quite edible, very mild, and highly nutritious. I always use them for my creamy broccoli soup.

Broccoli Stem Soup

2 cup broccoli stems, diced
1 cup red lentils, rinsed
6 cups water or vegetable broth
Salt and pepper to taste

Bring broccoli, water, salt, and pepper to a boil, then reduce to a simmer until lentils and broccoli are soft. Puree in a blender until creamy, and add more salt and/or pepper if needed.

Carrot Greens

Carrot greens have a reputation for being inedible. However, while it is true that carrot tops contain alkaloids and nitrates that some people may be sensitive to, they aren't inherently toxic to most of us unless we eat boatloads of them. Many times these greens end up in the compost — or worse, the trash — but there's no reason to waste these marvelous greens! Just always make sure to eat fresh and organic greens.

Carrot Greens Soup

½ yellow onion, chopped
1 large carrot, peeled and chopped
2 cups carrot greens, rinsed
3 cups vegetable broth
Salt and pepper to taste
½ cups raw cashews

Place everything except the cashews into a pot and bring to a boil. Cover and reduce to medium-low heat for 15 minutes. Spoon boiled ingredients plus the cashews into a blender and mix until creamy. Add more broth if the soup is too thick. Add salt and pepper to taste.

Leftover Coffee

First of all, congratulations if you're brewing your own cup of joe. You're already working on the most effortless and sustainable choice yet, especially if you're someone who barely can stay awake as you're making that cup of coffee. Now let's talk about why we should use leftover coffee.

Iced coffee cubes If, like me, you enjoy iced coffee, this is by far an easier way to make it. Pour leftover coffee into ice cube trays and freeze it. When you want iced coffee, simply pop a couple of coffee cubes into the milk of your choice. Yum!!!

Flavoring for baked goods You can add coffee to flavor any chocolate cakes and frostings. Just replace a couple of tablespoons of the liquid with the leftover coffee.

Composting is one of the most effective ways to reduce waste. An average family's waste bin contains 1/3 food waste, which produces methane as it decomposes.

Composting

Many people think that food you put in your trash will compost at the landfill. Unfortunately, that's just not true. In fact, it turns into methane gas which is almost twice as bad as carbon dioxide for the planet. Landfills don't have the proper environment for food to decompose in a useful way.

Composting isn't as hard as it sounds. There are different kinds of composting: bokashi composting, curbside composting, composting in an apartment, and traditional composting. Composting is a great way to reduce waste and turn food scraps into beautiful fertilizer.

Now, besides vegetable and fruit scraps, what else can be composted?

- Kitchen greens
- Corn husks and chopped up cobs
- Fruit pits and seeds
- Herbs and spices
- Tea leaves and natural paper tea bags — just make sure they are plastic free
- Coffee grounds
- Liquid filling from canned fruits and vegetables
- Crumbs
- Egg shells

- Cardboard egg cartons
- Unbleached coffee filters
- Brown paper shopping bags
- Cardboard food boxes
- Used paper napkins
- Cardboard pizza boxes
- Unbleached parchment paper
- Unwaxed and unbleached cupcake and muffin paper wrappers
- Uncoated paper plates
- Sawdust
- Newspapers
- Grass clippings
- Chicken poop
- Toothpicks
- Compostable toothbrushes
- Compostable dental floss
- Leaves
- Pet hair
- Human hair
- Dust bunnies
- Nail clippings
- Cotton, linen, and wool scraps
- Dryer lint
- Pencil shavings
- Junk mail
- Flowers from flower arrangements
- Fireplace ashes
- Christmas trees
- Bunny, gerbil and hamster bedding and poop (not dog or cat)
- Feathers

To learn more about composting see our chapter on Zero Waste Gardening.

Cooking from scratch is a great way to reduce food waste and save money. We love cooking together as a family and with friends.

Facts!

Fight climate change with diet change

Reduce your carbon footprint (or your "food-print") by reducing your meat consumption. Meat production account for approximately 14.5% of the world's greenhouse gases, 27% of all of humanity's usage and it is a major cause of deforestation of the rainforest. Additionally, 1,800 gallons of water is used per pound of beef produced.

So, you can fight climate change with your diet by following these methods.

• Eating less meat
• Eating more plant-based food
• Growing your own food
• Eating your own food
• Eating locally grown and produced food
• Eating organic food
• Reducing food waste

Source FoodPrint.org

We store our food without plastic by using beeswax wraps, reusable zip lock bags, stainless steel containers and Mason jars — a zero waster's best friend.

Storing Food Without Plastic

Is it possible to store food without plastic? *Absolutely!* The first thing I did when eliminating plastic was to search out glass food containers for storing cooked and raw leftover food in both the fridge and freezer. Then I got smart and started saving old Mason jars for food storage. Mason jars are perfect for freezing cooked beans or homemade tomato sauce in portions, and the large ones are great for storing soups and stews. When you're a zero waste family, you tend to become a hoarder of Mason jars because they're useful for so many things. We have also invested in some heavy-duty metal containers from Life Without Plastic. Metal food storage containers are also a great option for both fridge and freezer. The bonus of using metal is that food thaws quickly in a dish of hot water.

Photo Bee's Wrap®

We use reusable beeswax wraps instead of plastic wrap. These versatile wraps come in several sizes and you can use them for at least a year. And, they are compostable once they wear out.

Instead of using plastic wrap and foil, we now use Bee's Wrap and cloth bags. Beeswax wrap is a sheet made from 100% organic cotton fabric, natural beeswax, jojoba oil, coconut oil, and tree resin. It's a flexible wrap that is reusable (all you have to do is clean it in cold water). It clings like plastic wrap, so you can wrap food in it or cover a bowl. For snacks and sandwiches on-the-go, we use reusable sandwich bags I buy at the farmers market.

My husband James had a hard time letting go of zip lock bags, which I understand because they are so convenient. I searched a lot for a good functional replacement and was delighted when I found Stasher Bags (StasherBag.com) that work just like a zip lock bag — but they're reusable and made from food grade silicone. I use them for storing food and freezing vegetables and fruits from the garden. When I freeze bread, I use cloth bags. You can also use an old pillow case — it works like a charm. Once you start looking, you will find many great plastic-free food storage options, and you will be one step closer to a zero waste life!

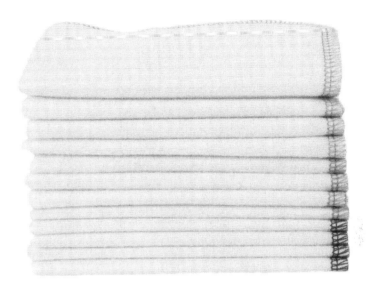

We use cloth towels instead of disposable paper towels to save trees and reduce waste. We keep a generous stack of them in a kitchen drawer that's easily accessible to the whole family.

Kitchen Hacks

Cloth Paper Towels

Many years ago, when I stopped using paper towels and decided to only use cloth ones, people thought I had lost my marbles. Here I was, a stay-at-home mom with a six-year-old, two-year-old, and a newborn… without paper towels. I'm so happy to have made that leap because not only have we saved many trees over the years, but we have also saved money. I always keep a generous stack of cloth paper towels in a kitchen drawer so they're easily accessible to both us parents and our kids. What I love most about them (besides being zero waste and kinder to the trees and our budget) is that they are hardcore and sturdy. I normally need only one towel for a big mess. And after I've cleaned around the house, I just toss them into the laundry hamper.

Cloth napkins look so much nicer than disposable ones – and they are much better for the environment! They can really dress up a table and last for years.

Reusable Napkins

Paper napkins are so convenient and useful; it can be hard to even think of giving them up. But I've managed to eliminate them since I started using cloth napkins. Not only are they fun and classy, but they are tough and absorbent enough for messy meals. When soiled, they just get tossed in the laundry hamper for the next wash. They are attractive and utilitarian and will last for many, many years. There are lots of great looking styles on Etsy.com

It's gratifying to see how many napkins we use each week, and I know we're making a difference.

Chapter 5

Mason Jars
(A Zero Waster's Best Friend)

"We do not inherit the earth from our ancestors.
We borrow it from our children."

– Wendell Berry

For a zero waste family, there is no such thing as too many Mason jars. They are great for so much: food storage, lunch boxes, smoothies, piggy banks for the kids, candle holders, vases, containers when buying bulk food, organizing dried foods in the pantry, housing homemade deodorant, and storing homemade household cleaners. The uses for Mason jars are endless, so having lots on hand when going zero waste is key.

The best part of jars is that you do not have to go buy brand new ones. Most of us have them already from foods we bought — or if you don't, put it out there to friends and family that you're looking for jars with lids, and they'll usually bring you some for free. I have found some nice bigger ones at thrift stores, too.

So, what do I use Mason jars for?

Food storage They are perfect for freezing cooked beans or homemade tomato sauce in portion sizes, and the large ones are great for storing soups and stews.

Homemade household cleaners They're perfect for storing household cleaners like citrus-scented cleaning vinegar and disinfectant wipes.

Personal hygiene products I make deodorant, toothpaste, and make-up remover and keep them in mason jars.

Bulk shopping—Skip the plastic bags and instead bring mason jars to fill and buy food in bulk.

Mason jars are great for storing food, but I also pre-make snacks in the smaller ones to keep handy for the kids to snack on.

Snacks on the go Pre-making foods and snacks in mason jars is a great way to facilitate eating well on-the-go. Making snacks in jars has been a healthy eating game-changer for my family and me. Having healthful, simple, easy-to-grab snacks on-hand in the fridge is a lifesaver for sure.

Bathroom organization They're great for storing cotton balls, Q-Tips, bath salts, powdered milk, extra toothbrushes, makeup brushes, combs, Band-Aids, etc. I keep a tiny two-ounce mason jar full of kitchen matches on the toilet tank to use as air deodorizers. The metal band of the two-piece lid serves as the strike strip.

Garage organization Store nails, screws, nuts, bolts, twine, washers, paint brushes, batteries, scraps of sandpaper, and all sorts of tiny miscellaneous hardware. Once again, the clear glass will make it easy to spot just what you need. You can store excess dry cat or dog food as well.

Gift giving A simple and inexpensive way to wrap gifts! Simply put your gift inside the mason jar and finish it off with an oversized ribbon tied around the glass to keep your recipients wondering what's inside.

How to remove labels from mason jars

When you recycle old mason jars to use again most of the jars come with labels that

Mason jars are great for packing meals to bring to school, work, or play. They are leakproof and can be heated in the microwave.

can be challenging to remove. Here are my tips for removing stubborn labels:

- Fill your sink or a large bowl with hot water
- Add 2 tablespoons dish soap and ½ cup of white vinegar
- Soak jars for 20-30 minutes
- Remove jars from water and remove labels
- If there are still sticky glue left, use a few drops of lemon essential oil and scrub with a dish rag or scrub brush
- Wash and dry jars, and they're ready to use!

Meals

One of my favorite tricks is using Mason jars for packing meals. They're great for bringing food to school; the jars are basically leak-proof and can also be heated up in microwave ovens. Because they are made from glass, there is no risk of leaching chemicals as plastic does. The only downside is that they are a little heavy; but this doesn't have to be a problem, especially if you use a cooler, lunch box, or have a fridge to store them in during the day. Almost anything can be packed into a Mason jar and brought to work, school, or wherever the day takes you.

Layered salads are one of our favorite Mason jar meals – complete with dressing – ready to pour in a bowl or eat straight from the jar.

Here are some of my favorite Mason jar meals

Salad in a Jar

I use a quart sized jar for a full salad, complete with dressing, ready to pour into a bowl or eat right out of the jar. The basic idea is that the greens don't get soggy from sitting in dressing for a few hours because of the way the ingredients are layered! Here is an example of one of my favorite salads to bring to school and how to add its ingredients to the jar.

DIY Salad in a Jar

1. On the bottom of the jar, put 1-2 tablespoons of your favorite dressing or simply a good quality olive oil and vinegar. Mix balsamic vinegar with a bit of strong mustard, raw honey, olive oil, and salt.

2. Put in a handful of nuts or seeds. The hardness of the ingredients make them able to withstand sitting in salad dressing for a while.

3. Add hard fruits or vegetables. Chopped cauliflower, broccoli, apples, squash, carrots, persimmons, cabbage or any other tough food could be used. They also will marinate a little bit in the dressing on the bottom and won't be any worse for wear.

4. After that, add softer items — tomatoes, avocado, cucumbers, cheese, sprouts, rice or beans, for example. These things might get a little exposure to dressing if the jar is tossed around a bit in transit, but they won't get soggy or soft.

5. For the top layer, add your greens! Don't fill it all the way to the top because you need room to shake and combine. The greens will be kept away from the dressing, and stay fresh and crisp until you're ready to eat. My favorite greens to add are arugula, baby kale or romaine lettuce.

6. Before eating, give the jar a good shake and transfer the salad to a nice big bowl, or shake it even harder to get dressing on everything and eat right out of the jar!

Burrito Bowl in a Jar

Either a quart jar or a pint jar would work for this recipe, depending on your other meals and how hungry you are. The salsa serves as a sort of dressing for this meal, but additional salsa or sour cream could be added!

DIY Burrito Bowl in a Jar

1. On the bottom of the jar, add already cooked rice, quinoa, or another grain.
2. Next, layer some already cooked black beans or pinto beans.
2. Throw in chopped bell pepper, tomato, thawed sweet corn, or onion.
4. Add a thin layer of chopped avocado or guacamole.
5. And your favorite salsa on top of that.
6. Include your greens as the top layer, and you're ready to go!

Almond Butter Overnight Oats

1 large ripe/spotty banana, mashed
2 tbsp. chia seeds
1 tbsp. almond butter (or peanut butter)
½ cup gluten free rolled oats
¾ cup almond milk
½ vanilla bean: slice open and scrape out seeds

1. Mash the banana in a small bowl with the vanilla bean until smooth.
2. Stir in the chia seeds until combined.
3. Add the oats, almond milk and almond butter, and blend until well mixed.
4. Pour into a mason jar and screw the lid on.
5. Refrigerate overnight.
6. Before eating, stir the oats to combine.

Chia Pudding with Fruit in a Jar

1 cup milk of your choice
1 ½ tbsp chia seeds
1 tbs maple syrup
pinch of vanilla bean

1. Combine milk, vanilla, chia seeds and maple syrup in a food processor or blender, and mix for 1 minute.

2. Using a pint-sized Mason jar, spread a layer of chia pudding on the bottom.

3. Next, add a mixture of fresh or frozen berries, mango pieces, kiwi, or sliced bananas.

4. Add another layer of chia.

5. Top with more fruit.

6. If you want some more texture, add a handful of chopped nuts, cacao nibs, trail mix, or granola!

7. Place in the fridge for a couple of hours or overnight.

Chapter 6
Zero Waste Gardening

"The world is changed by your example, not your opinion."

– Paulo Coelho, *Brazilian lyricist*

I have talked a lot about zero waste life, which, of course, means that nothing gets sent to a landfill and that we live according to the following principles: refuse, reduce, reuse, rot, and recycle. This works in the home, but did you know that you also can garden the zero waste way? This is what my family now does. No matter if you grow food or flowers in your garden, the goal is to cleverly reuse and upcycle items to significantly reduce garden waste as well. As a bonus, you save money.

In 2016, we turned our backyard on a normal city lot — 1/8 of an acre, 10 minutes from downtown San Diego — into a vegetable garden. Our plan was to grow as much food as possible to feed our family of five the very best that is also package free and sustainably grown. It's a huge part of our zero waste lifestyle. For most of the year we, grow all the vegetables we eat, and we usually grow more than we eat. So we preserve some for later. It feels amazing to only go grocery shopping for bulk foods like rice, pasta, flour, beans, lentils, spices, nuts, seeds, and oats.

Basically, today, we grow food pretty much everywhere except for an area reserved for our children's swing set, sandbox, and trampoline. We grow about 35 different vegetables and herbs and 15 different fruits and berries throughout the year. Basically, growing your own food indoors or on a patio — even just a few herbs in a garden — is sustainable food and makes a difference, besides tasting way better than anything you can buy. And, if you can grow your food without waste, even better.

You can make your own worm compost bin super easy and fast from two plastic storage bins.

Here are my tips for zero waste gardening

Soil You can keep improving soil by adding lots of mulch and compost. This way, you do not need to continually buy soil. Compost will add microorganisms. Adding grass clippings, leaves, and discarded plant materials will increase its fertility. And there's not a way to add too much organic matter to your soil. In fact, if you grow your soil, the plants grow themselves.

Seeds If you're part of a garden community or have joined a Facebook garden group, the odds are that people are offering free seeds or seedlings or will happily trade. There are also seed libraries, so check around for them and, of course, save your own seeds for replanting. I have previously shared a blog post about making your own seedling pots from upcycled materials like milk cartons and toilet rolls.

Water Rain water is free, so take advantage of harvesting it. For us, who grow food in San Diego's hot climate, rain harvesting is a great way to be water wise. You can reduce water usage by 50% by installing a graywater system that collects and cleans water from your shower, sink and washing machine, then transports it into the garden.

Another way we made our garden water wise, and therefore saved lots of money, was to remove all the grass, then plant either garden boxes or succulents that one of our neighbors was giving away. We also water all of our fruit trees with gray water from our washing machine. My husband created a very simple gray water system himself.

Compost is the key to a healthy and thriving garden. Why spend money buying compost when you can make for it free with zero waste?

Mulch I always smile when I hear how much money people spend on mulch when it's usually free somewhere in your neighborhood. We use grass clippings, weeds and leaves from our garden as well as from our neighbors who we know do not use chemicals, and old plants as mulch. Adding mulch around your plants helps reduce evaporation and cools the soil. Good mulch actually can help reduce a plant's water needs by as much as 50%. Add about 1-3 inches of mulch. You will be amazed how fast mulch will break down, which actually adds nutrients to the soil.

Planter boxes and pots Look for recycled materials to use as plant containers, and free wood and boxes online. Old wood pallets are usually found for free, and they are great for making bed edging for new raised beds. Furthermore, wood pallets are great for creative vertical gardens for a south-facing wall. We have found lots of pots, planters, old wood, etc., to use for building boxes and planting plants in. If you choose pallet wood, just make sure that you know what the pallets were used for and if they were treated with chemicals that you do not want in your garden.

Mulch protects plants, adds nutrition to the soil, and helps reduce water use. We use fallen leaves, hay, and grass clippings.

Fertilizer Compost is the very best fertilizer, as I said, a key for growing seeds, soil and plants. Another free fertilizer is bunny and guinea pig poop. Unlike other animal poop, bunny and guinea pig poop does not need to be composted first in order to be used in garden beds. We're lucky to have a bunny doing his part to help fertilize the garden. If you don't have one of these pets, I bet you know someone who does and might be happy to give you some.

Calcium powder Calcium powder raises the PH of soil. Tomatoes especially need that in order to grow healthy fruit. We make our own calcium powder by first boiling egg shells, then drying them in a 350°F oven until completely dry. After that, we grind them into a powder in a mixer.

Compost Homemade compost is the key for growing healthy and nutrient dense vegetables. I always say start composting before starting a garden. Compost enriches the soil, helps it retain moisture, and suppresses plant diseases and pests. It also reduces the need for chemical fertilizers.

Sure you can buy compost, but why should you when creating your own is so easy and free. Plus, composting your organic waste also helps reduce your waste, so it's a win-win, right?

Growing your own food in your garden makes you appreciate food more, and it's a good way to eat healthy and sustainably.

You can compost simply by using the dig and drop method

1. Dig a hole, approximately 10 to 12 inches deep and as wide as you want or need it to be.
2. Drop food scraps or other organic matter into the hole.
3. Replace the soil, and you're finished.

We have a garden compost heap, which is where we combine garden discards and chicken poop, which has to be composted before being used as fertilizer. For our garden compost, we built a simple wooden bin in a corner. We also compost using a worm bin that we made ourselves from two storage bins together with our kids and it works great.

How to Make a Worm-Composting Bin From Plastic Buckets Simple 2-Bucket System

What you need

- Two equal-sized plastic bins (that can stack inside each other) with 1 bucket lid
- Drill with 3/16 and 1/8-inch twist bits
- Brick of Coconut Coir or Shredded newspaper and cardboard
- 250 to 500 Red wiggler composting worms
- 4 small blocks

Fun Fact

Food scraps and yard waste together currently make up more than 30 percent of what we throw away and could be composted instead. Making compost keeps these materials out of landfills where they take up space and release methane, a potent greenhouse gas.

Prepare the bins

- Drill 8-16 holes in the bottom of one bin.
- Drill another 10-20 holes on the side of that same bin just under the lid.
- Place the 4 small blocks in the corner of the bin without holes, place the bin with holes in
    the other bin (on top of the blocks).

Prepare the bedding

- Hydrate the Coconut Coir in the bucket with holes (or add your shredded newspaper and cardboard).
- The bedding should be moist but not dripping wet.
- Add the worms to the inner bin.
- Add food.
- Mix food scraps into the bedding the next day (see tips below).

Tips for a healthy worm bin

- Feed the worms 1–2 times per week. Make sure they've eaten through most of the food you previously added before adding more. If you have more food than the worms can eat then add more worms.
- Pro tip: I will put the food scraps in a food processor before putting it on the worm bin. The worms will eat through the food much faster!
- Keep your worm bin somewhere that is shaded most/all of the day. Keep the environment moist (but not dripping wet). If the worm bin dries out, the worms will die. Add water if you need to, but food will also add moisture.

Tip for reducing odors

- Remove liquid that drains into the bottom bin. This is called 'compost tea,' it is filled with nutrients and can be added directly to your garden.

If the bin attract animals

- Keep your worm bin sealed and it should not attract small critters.
- If ants find their way into your worm bin, make sure all the food sits below the surface.

Pesticides and insecticides — You never want to use any harsh chemicals to eliminate bugs in your garden, so we primarily use castile soap to fight off most common bugs. We also employ essential oils like cinnamon bark, peppermint and Thieves oil. All you need is a glass spray bottle, water, and a few drops of essential oils. Another method of fighting pests is companion planting, and you can find lots of information about that on the internet.

Another Great Homemade Pesticide is Pepper Spray

Pepper Spray for Plants

2 cups water
1 cup hot peppers
  or 2 tbsp cayenne pepper
¼ onion
6 cloves of garlic

Another method of fighting pests is companion planting and you can lots of information about that on the web

Blend peppers and water in a blender, strain it through a milk or nut bag, making sure to wear gloves. Separate the juice from pulp, add to a spray bottle and add 1 tbsp castle soap. Shake before using. Spray will last 2–3 weeks in refrigerator. Wash vegetables before eating.

Homemade Weed Killer

You'll need:
1 gallon white vinegar
1 cup Epsom salt

1. Stir salt and water until completely dissolved.
2. Add 1 tbsp Castile soap.
3. Do not apply to plants you're growing because it will kill them.
4. It does not affect the soil.
5. Apply every couple of weeks.

Our garden is a family affair. It's also a classroom where our children learn biology, math, science, and nutrition We grow our own food to make sure our children eat healthier and sustainably.

My Tips for Getting Children Interested in Gardening

Our garden is a family affair and the whole family helps out. It's not always easy to interest our children in the activities we enjoy; it's the same with gardening. But it is something beautiful and simple that can bring families closer while enjoying the outdoors. In our case, gardening also feeds our family. Our main goal with our homestead, besides growing our own food, is to work together and spend quality time together.

Let kids choose what to plant – Kids feel empowered when they can make decisions. Offer guidance and make sure there are some successful, thriving plants among their selection. But listen to their ideas, and let them play and experiment. Our kids each have a fruit tree they helped plant. They love to share figs from Noah's tree and peaches from Bella's.

Don't expect perfection – This is the time to get dirty and messy, to connect with the earth, and feel the dirt between your fingers. Getting dirty in the garden is a great way to boost the immune system anyway. Don't worry about the result or how neat it looks.

Give them a task or make them a helper– Kids love to feel special, and when you give them something to oversee, they feel you trust them. It can be something simple like watering or dropping seeds into holes you dug together. Mix up the tasks to keep it interesting. My boys love to help me plant, so I dig the hole and they put the plant into it and place soil around it.

Fun Fact

Growing your own food is not only delicious, but it also has nutritional and environmental benefits. Unlike supermarket-bought produce, it does not require transportation, therefore retaining nutritional value that would be lost during the time taken to move the fruits or vegetables to a supermarket. Since homegrown food does not need to be packaged, it's a great way to reduce waste at home.

Be creative – Allow them to create their own plant markers or garden ornaments. They can paint on stones or popsicle sticks and put them next to the plant. Another idea is to plant gardens with a theme, like "rainbow," where you plant items of one color in different sections so that when they bloom, they turn into a rainbow of various colors. Another theme is a pizza garden of tomatoes, basil, garlic and oregano. Children will love planning meals when they harvest the fruits.

Read books—Nothing like reading books about gardening or composting makes the kids more aware and interested. My kids' favorite books include these:

- Composting: Nature's Recycling
- The Ugly Vegetable Garden
- Gardening Projects for Kids
- Pee Wee at Castle Compost

Gardening is therapy. It helps you relax, it feeds your soul, and connects you with food and the planet. So invite your kids to play and discover this, too! Start slowly, and give your children lots of encouragement. Once you share your enthusiasm and passion for gardening, your flowers and vegetables are not the only things that will blossom.

Chapter 7

Zero Waste
Arts and Crafts

*"Quality of time is more important than quantity of time. But with kids,
quantity of time is often needed for those moments of quality time."*

*— **James Harker-Syren**, Zero Waste Dad*

Since we do not buy many toys, our kids tend to either spend lots of time playing outdoors or doing arts and crafts.

Surprisingly, lots of children's arts and crafts materials contain harmful chemicals, preservatives, and synthetics. Children put art materials on their skin, and some also put them into their mouths. It's a fact that arts and crafts materials almost never include lists of their ingredients — and many common products contain petrochemicals and heavy-metal-based pigments. The most common toxins found in children's paints are lead, cadmium, and formaldehyde. It's also a fact that children's arts and crafts paints are exempt from consumer paint lead laws. That's crazy to me because the risks of lead exposure for children are common knowledge.

To reduce waste as well as our carbon footprint, we keep chemicals away from our children, buy craft and art papers that are 100% recycled, and use paint and art supplies that are both chemical-free and minimally packaged.

My kids absolutely love face paints and will spend hours painting each other's faces. This is another reason to use all organic and natural ingredients.

Here's a list of my favorite chemical-free art and craft supplies

Natural Earth Paint Natural paints in powder form to be mixed with a little water. Very easy to use. (naturalearthpaint.com)

Eco-kid Art pads, play dough, crayons, and finger paints made with nontoxic, natural ingredients. Made in the US and packed in environmental-friendly material. (ecokidsusa.com)

Earth Grown Crayons Eco-friendly crayons made from 100% biodegradable soy and packaged in recycled and reusable materials. (earthgrowncrayons.com)

Lots of children's arts and crafts materials contain harmful chemicals, preservatives, and synthetics; so make sure to use only chemical-free supplies.

Stockmar Sells watercolors, pencils, and crayons that are certified nontoxic by the Art and Crafts Materials Institute. (stockmar.de/en/)

Veggie Baby Sells quality dough, paint sets, dyes, chalk, and crayons made from fruits and vegetable powders. All products are plant-based, natural, and made without chemicals, preservatives, or color additives. (veggiebaby.com)

Earth Hero Sells sidewalk chalk, finger paints, crayons, water colors, and more. They contain only natural and organic fruit, plant, and vegetable extracts. Powdered paints come in recyclable paper cartons. Packaging is printed with soy inks on FSC Certified Paper in a wind-powered factory. (earthhero.com)

Here are recipes for my favorite homemade arts and crafts supplies

Homemade Soap Bubbles

6 cups of water
2 cups of Dawn dish soap
3/4 cup corn syrup

Slowly combine all ingredients in a large bowl. Let sit for at least an hour, but overnight is better.

Play Dough with Essential Oil

2 cups of flour
1 cups of salt
2 tsp cream of tartar
2 tlsp oil
2 cups of cold water

A few drops of any essential oil
optional food coloring (*I use spirulina powder, but beets, blueberry powder, or turmeric can be used*)
Don't worry—This won't stain!

Mix flour, salt, cream of tartar, oil, and water in a medium saucepan. Stir over medium heat for about 5 minutes, until play dough reaches the right consistency. Allow to coll, then split into 3 ball and knead in essential oils and optional food coloring until evenly distributed throughout each ball of dough. Store in an airtight container.

Colored Epsom salt art is a super easy natural craft to do with kids that only requires natural colors, usually found at home, and Epsom salt.

Colored Epsom Salts I don't know how or from whom I learned this, but my daughter particularly loves this craft and has so much fun with it. Basically, you need a spoon, a glass jar, Epsom salts, and food coloring. Blend the salts with a few drops of food coloring. You want to make a few different colors so you can mix and layer them. Place each colored salt into a different bowl, then give the artist a spoon for pouring salt mixes into a glass jar to create fun color patterns.

So many arts and crafts supplies can be made at home, including sidewalk paint. It's a lot of fun to do with kids - and saves money!

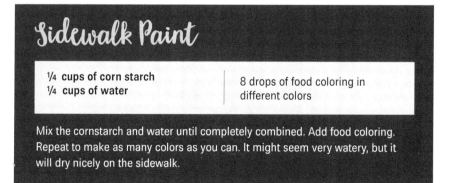

Sidewalk Paint

¼ **cups of corn starch** ¼ **cups of water**	8 drops of food coloring in different colors

Mix the cornstarch and water until completely combined. Add food coloring. Repeat to make as many colors as you can. It might seem very watery, but it will dry nicely on the sidewalk.

If you have kids, you have broken pieces of crayons - easily made into new crayons.

Recycling Old Crayons

Broken and old crayons Flexible molds or muffin papers Cookie sheet	For the molds, you can fun different shapes such as hearts, etc. (*Inexpensive silicon molds are sold at Ikea*)

Directions Remove the paper around crayons by either picking it off or slicing sideways over the paper with a sharp knife. (*The step is best for adults to perform*)

Preheat oven to 250°F

Chop the nubs into small pieces.

Put pieces into molds. You can either mix colors for fun tie-dye effects or sort crayons into colors

Place molds on a cookie sheet and put in oven until crayons melt, about 15-20 minutes.

Let cool completely before carefully removing them from molds.

Chapter 8

Zero Waste Parties

"If you want your children to turn out well, spend twice as much time with them and half as much money."

– Abigail Van Buren, "Dear Abby"

W hile it might be hard to imagine a birthday party without the endless mountain of plates, cups, napkins, uneaten food, gift wrap, gift boxes, and disposable decorations, I'm here to tell you that it's possible.

For our birthday parties, we try our best to maintain our zero waste lifestyle without sacrificing the celebratory fun for each birthday kid. While it does require a bit more work and DIY energy in the planning phase, sticking to your zero waste lifestyle even in the midst of celebrating is completely possible. In fact, our zero waste parties have become so popular that we now have a zero waste party box that contains reusable plates, napkins, cups, pitchers, and utensils that we lend out to other families from school. Who knows? You might just create a ripple effect.

Tips for throwing a Zero Waste party

1. **Send paperless invitations**

   Paper invitations waste trees and natural resources, so one option is to use only those made from 100% recycled paper. Some good options for sending an electronic invitation are Paperless Post or evite.com.

2. **Skip the paper plates, plastic cups, bowls, napkins, etc.**

   Disposable dishware and utensils may be more convenient, but they'll end up in a landfill after the party. Instead, we use our regular plates and glasses. Yes, that means more dishes to clean afterward— but nothing is more wasteful than disposable products. We also skip straws for that same reason.

Skip disposables and use real plates, cups, and napkins for parties to reduce waste and save money. Don't forget to compost any leftovers, too.

3. Use natural and reusable decorations

Let imaginations run wild and let the kids help out by making paper signs, use plants, flowers, twigs, leaves, and fabric to decorate the house for the party. All you really need are fun colors.

4. Buy eco-friendly balloons

My boys love balloons. I think most kids do. Heck, I still do. There is just something fun about batting them around and popping them. For the best green options, make sure to get latex balloons that are 100% biodegradable and compostable – mylar balloons end up in the landfill.

5. Make fun organic and healthy treats

I'm lucky—my kids love pancakes— so many of our parties have been pancake-themed. We serve different flavored pancakes (vegan and gluten-free options included) along with cream, fruits, berries, jam, and syrup — a guaranteed hit. For the more traditional parties with cake, I offer snacks like veggies and hummus, fruit with yogurt dip, smoothies, and homemade lemonade. I always make the cake because it's super easy and much cheaper.

6. Serve homemade drinks and bring water

Avoid juice packages because they are not recyclable and come with plastic straws. Instead, make homemade drinks like lemonade or buy large glass bottles of apple cider, apple juice, or grape juice and avoid plastic bottles! Also, provide a water station where guests can refill their own reusable bottles and ask them to bring their own.

Make a themed party. My kids love pancakes, so instead of cakes, they love a pancake party with a variety of pancakes, syrups, and lots of berries and fruits.

7. Encourage

Encourage guests to save on wrapping paper by implementing reusable wooden boxes or sheets of newspaper along with natural string and ribbons. Don't be shy, put it on the invitation!

8. Make a green goodie bag

Forget the plastic toys and packaged candy. Instead, use paper bags made from recycled paper and have the birthday kid help decorate the bags with color before filling them with seeds for planting, homemade goodies, or moldable beeswax (my kids' favorite).

9. Plan fun activities

At our parties, we almost always do some sort of craft, such as making personalized lanterns out of old jars or planters that each child can take home. We also might do some painting if we're feeling wild. My son Noah loves soccer, so we will have a soccer party in the park so he and his friends can play a friendly game. Our kids also really enjoy scavenger hunts where they have to work together figuring out clues that will bring them to the treasure (which can be a treat or goodie bag).

Rather than deflating the life out of a happening party, I have a hunch you'll find that going zero waste has the opposite effect — it can actually free you up to have a little more fun and focus on what really matters.

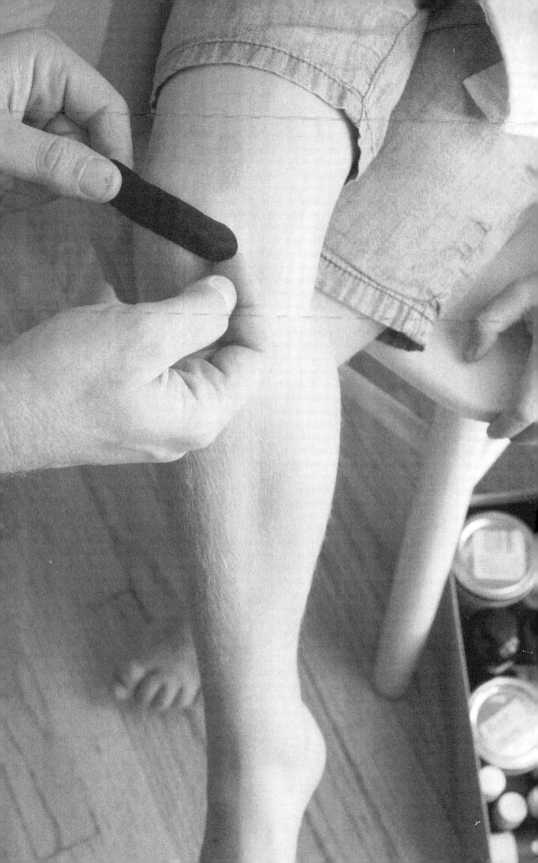

Chapter 9

Zero Waste First-Aid Kit

"There is no such thing as 'away'. When we throw anything away it must go somewhere."

*– **Annie Leonard**, American proponent of sustainability*

With children come bumps, scrapes, and cuts — so, naturally, most parents have a first-aid kit or drawer. We do, too. However, we have taken the extra step to make it as zero waste as possible.

First, what to store all the supplies in? This largely depends on the amount of items you choose to include. For instance, you can reuse the clear plastic zip pouches that often contain a gift pedicure set. They come in handy for travel and keep liquid items separated. You could use a travel toiletry organizer, metal box, Tupperware container, shoe box, or just a canvas tote bag. We keep our first-aid supplies in an old shoe box.

To maintain your zero waste lifestyle while putting together your first-aid kit, it's helpful to be come familiar with basic wound care: clean the wound thoroughly with soap and warm water, let it air dry, apply antiseptic as needed, then wrap with a sterile dressing. For minor scrapes, you can simply wash with soap and water for at least 15 seconds, rinse thoroughly, and then let air dry. This can be just as effective as using alcohol wipes or other antiseptics. Store ointments, powders, and salves in small glass jars or metal tins that can be washed and refilled as needed.

The Essentials

- Scraps of organic cotton or silk (I cut scraps from old t-shirts)
- Band-Aids are almost never biodegradable, so we use activated charcoal bandages that are both compostable and biodegradable
- Cotton balls

Every household should have a first aid kit.to be prepared – just in case. We have one, too, but have made an effort to make ours with as little waste as possible.

- Ace bandage
- Soap
- Tweezers
- Thermometer

Young Living essential oils for kids:

- KidScents Owie — apply to bumps and bruises
- KidScents TummyGize — helps soothes tummy aches
- KidScents SniffleEase — a few drops under the nose helps a stuffy nose
- Lavender essential oil — helps with rashes and burns
- Thieves and Tee Tree oil — for cleaning wounds

To store in glass jars

- Manuka honey (great natural antibacterial and antiseptic)
- Aloe vera gel (for burns and bites)
- Hydrogen peroxide and/or iodine (antiseptic)
- Elderberry syrup (boosts natural immunity to cold and flu viruses)

It's important to learn basic wound care and first-aid treatment and to learn what natural products you can use to treat normal cuts and scrapes.

To store in metal tins

- Burt's Bees Res-Q Ointment — for insect bites and rashes
- Calendula salve — for skin inflammation, sunburn relief, bug bite itch relief, burns, & diaper rash
- Bentonite clay — for poison ivy rash (apply as a paste to dry the rash out). Look for this locally - not in plastic.
- Digize essential oils — helps with digestive upset, nausea, motion sickness, and morning sickness. Any time our kids get a stomach ache, they get a couple drops mixed with water
- Lavender Essential oil — for scrapes and burns
- Acetaminophen, ibuprofen, aspirin, children's Motrin, or Tylenol

Chapter 10
Zero Waste Clothes

*"Every time you spend money, you are casting
a vote for the world you want."*

– Anna Lappe

The clothing industry is the second-largest polluter in the world and second-largest when it comes to water use. Almost 2,000 different harmful chemicals like formaldehyde, chlorine, lead, and mercury are used to produce textiles. Most of the chemicals are used for the dyeing process.

To live more sustainably and reduce waste, you should make a few changes when it comes to how and where you buy clothes. If everyone got into the habit of coming up with clever ways to reduce, reuse, repurpose, repair, and recycle old textiles, the clothing industry would be more sustainable.

The Five R's of Fashion

1. Reduce

It's completely possible to achieve a high-fashion look with less. One great way to do so is by investing in a capsule wardrobe, which is a compact wardrobe consisting of around thirty or fewer high-quality staple pieces in coordinating colors. This includes shoes and sometimes accessories. It's a minimalist principle of fashion that saves money, the planet, space, and time. Looking fabulous with a minimal wardrobe and using less waste is an eco-friendly way of living.

2. Reuse

This one, of course, is easy—you simply say "no" to buying more clothing. But the truth is that it's difficult to do. We all want to look good — and we still can, even when saying "no." First, make sure to buy quality over quantity so your clothes

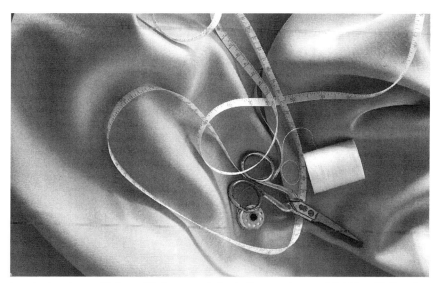

Learning how to mend holes and fix loose or missing buttons can be a useful skill, and believe it or not, can be surprisingly fun!

will last longer. Second, take extra care of your clothes by washing them in water of the right temperature, hanging them to dry, and taking care of stains right away. Taking these measures will help make your clothes last for a long time.

3. Recycle

When you grow tired of certain pieces, don't just throw them away! You have a couple of options. First, try selling your unwanted, but still-in-good-condition clothing. I have sold lots of my clothes on eBay or to local second-hand stores. You can also donate! Your clothes might be perfect for someone else.

4. Repurpose

You can find tips for repurposing old clothes on both Pinterest and YouTube.

5. Repair

If your garment is missing a button, learn how to sew it back on. If a zipper is broken, learn how to fix it. If there is a small hole or stain, learn how to cover it the fashionable way. And it's a good skill to know how to mend holes in socks.

Eco-chic with Slow Fashion

When you hear the words "fast food," what comes to mind? Probably cheap, unhealthy, and perhaps even bad for the planet. Now, think about "fast fashion" compared to "slow fashion". This concept actually makes sense. Over the years, we have come to accept the quickly-changing fashion trends that come with a market of inexpensive knock-offs. In today's society, we want to spend less money on more things, and, unfortunately, this has a devastating effect on the planet.

Just as fast and cheap foods come from factory farms where the animals are treated badly, fast fashion is usually manufactured overseas in sweatshops and factories with unfair working conditions. In 2013, for example, 2,000 people in Bangladesh were making clothes for a large western brand when the factory collapsed and more than 1,100 people were killed. Fast clothing trends come with mass production that uses lots of chemicals and pesticides — which creates waste. For example, water reservoirs are increasingly diminished for cotton crop irrigation, and other precious natural resources are being wasted. Sounds like factory food production, right?

Instead of supporting the damaging effects of fast fashion, we should look for production that is local, sustainable, high-quality, and slow. Why should we look to buy locally produced clothes? Not only does locally manufactured clothing (generally speaking) ensure a better work environment, but it also reduces the carbon footprint caused by fossil fuels and transportation. The slow fashion movement also looks at the importance of designing, creating, and purchasing garments for quality and longevity. It also encourages smaller carbon footprints and (ideally) zero waste. Slow fashion encourages consumers to become more aware of the entire process of making clothes — from design to production to potential reuse (which is becoming more popular as well).

The slow fashion movement is growing, and it's all about becoming mindful of the process of making clothes and knowing who's making them, as well as where they're made. Slow fashion means slowing down to make sure clothes are made with care and with less impact on the planet. The slow fashion movement is steadily gaining momentum, and I believe it is here to stay as people are getting more into eco-friendly and ethical fashion trends.

Fact!

It takes nearly 2,000 gallons of water to make a pair of jeans, equivalent to the amount of water the average person drinks over a period seven years.

Source: United Nations Report, March 2019

An average fleece item can shed 1.7 grams of tiny plastic bits, also known as microfibers, or micro plastics, per wash.

Here are some of my favorite Slow Fashion Brands

Patagonia makes quality clothing with organic, recycled, and up-cycled fibers. Their clothing packs well, travels even better, lasts forever, and feels good to wear.

Eileen Fisher makes high-quality working clothes for women while quietly but persistently increasing the number of organic fibers they use. Their style is elegant, comfortable, and hardworking.

Kowtow is a brand from New Zealand that makes certified, fair trade, organic clothing that is ethically and sustainably made, from seed to garment.

United By Blue For every product sold, the company will remove one pound of trash from oceans and waterways. They manufacture organic cotton, and their clothes and backpacks are awesome.

Blue Canoe makes everyday-wear organic cotton and bamboo clothing that really works for women.

Alternative Apparel makes a good basic shirt that is also sustainable.

Brook There makes sexy, comfortable, and organic underwear.

Synergy creates lovely, organic dresses and yoga-wear that benefit women in Nepal.

Are Your Jeans Damaging The Planet?

Making one pair of stonewashed jeans requires an additional 500 gallons of water. On top of this, cotton is being used as one of its major raw materials, and cotton production relies on lots of pesticides that pollute our soil, water and planet. The fact is that up to 2,000 different harmful chemicals like formaldehyde, chlorine, lead and mercury are used to produce textiles. Most of the chemicals are used for the dyeing process. Take denim for example. Most of us own at least one pair of denims and use them all the time. Most denim jeans are produced in China, and today the waterways around the factories in China are blue — not natural "water blue" but the blue of all the harmful denim dyes and chemicals.

 The good news is that the fashion industry is beginning to answer the demand for more sustainable fashion, so today more denim jeans producers rely on recycled materials like plastic or even old denim to make new jeans. Some manufacturers are committed to finding new ways to produce their garments with less water and less impact on the planet.

Although there are more eco-friendlier denim jeans brands than ever, the truth is that if you want to be truly sustainable, buying used jeans is the best option. I have found great deals on used jeans at Thredup.com. But if you want used jeans and can't find them, here are some of the most ethical and eco-friendly denim jeans brands.

San Francisco-based Levi Strauss & Co. has been a transcendent leader and is an icon. It's great to see that this successful company is still trying to break the boundaries. Today their trademarked Water<Less innovations have saved more than 1.8 billion liters of water and recycled more than 129 million liters of water. Furthermore, they also have the Waste<Less™ collection of products made of 20% post-consumer waste — specifically, recycled plastic bottles. That works out to an average of three to eight plastic bottles per pair. Since 2013, this initiative has used 11.9 million recycled bottles for jeans products such as Levi's® 511™ Skinny jeans, Levi's® Trucker jackets and the women's Levi's® Boyfriend Skinny jeans.

G-Star — This denim jeans brand uses organic and recycled cotton, and also includes Better Cotton in its material mix. They are also using innovative dyeing and finishing processes that include ozone bleaching, laser treatments, and natural tanning of leather, which have a reduced social and environmental impact.

Source Denim — This denim jeans brand is produced in the USA. They work on developing new ways of making denim, replacing toxic chemicals with an all-natural material that cuts the number of chemicals in a pair of blue jeans in half, and uses 60%

less water and 40% less energy than ordinary denim production. They are also trying to close the loop on old denim jeans ending up in landfills by offering to take back all denim (even denim that's theirs) to be recycled into building insulation or rugs.

Kuyichi — This denim brand manufactures jeans with 100% organic cotton and recycled cotton as well as recycled polyester and hemp, as they try to rely on sustainable materials only. The jeans are washed with sustainable ozone and laser techniques that save lots of water and reduce the use of chemicals.

Plastic Pollution From Clothes

I love fleece and used to favor clothes and blankets made with it. Fleece is great— it's light, warm, cheap, and great for staying warm in the middle of winter. So, what's the problem with fleece? The sad truth is that fleece is plastic pollution.

A study by researchers at the University of California found that an average fleece jacket can shed 1.7 grams of tiny plastic bits, also known as microfibers (or microplastics) per wash. Older fleece items shed the most — almost double the amount. Microplastic is plastic debris less than five millimeters long (about the size of a sesame seed). Unfortunately, these tiny plastic pieces then travel out to a local wastewater plant where 40% of them end up in rivers, lakes, and oceans — becoming one of the worst plastic polluters. Because of its size, it's hard to clean up. For example, the Great Lakes, which comprise one-fifth of the world's fresh water — are polluted with billions of microscopic plastic particles. They are found by skimming the surface with finely meshed netting dragged behind sailing vessels. The same scientists who have studied gigantic masses of floating plastic in the Pacific Ocean are now reporting massive amounts of plastic in the Great Lakes.

Synthetic microfibers are particularly harmful to marine life that eat them as they mistake them for food. Once consumed, these small pieces of plastic transfer toxins and pesticides into the bodies of marine life. They also linger in our eco-systems, eventually spreading to us or other animals. Scientists and environmentalists are not sure how to remove these microbeads from the water because of their size, so the plastic accumulates in the water. Instead of fleece, fibers like organic wool and cotton are the better option.

Recycling Old Clothes

Until a couple of years ago, I did not know about textile production's effect on our planet.

The sad part is that most old clothes and textiles will eventually end up in a landfill. About 11.1 million tons of textiles such as t-shirts, pants, blankets, tablecloths, sheets, and baby clothes are thrown into the trash and then into landfills each year in the United States.

What's the solution? Reusing and recycling old things — thereby preventing them from going into the landfill — are great ways to reduce the use of raw materials and energy, air pollution, water pollution, waste, and greenhouse emissions. The next time you have a bag of old textiles, take a moment to research where you can donate and keep them out of the landfill, because ruined and stained textiles do not belong in landfills. Currently, textiles account for 5.2% of the waste in landfills. According to the Environmental Protection Agency (EPA), the average person discards 70 pounds of clothing per year (despite the fact that there are recyclers who accept all fabrics in various conditions).

The good news is that today there are many zero waste and eco-friendly ways to discard your old clothes — even your undergarments and socks!

1. **Donate** A great option for clean and unwanted clothes is to donate them to secondhand shops. Make sure that you donate only wearable clothes in good condition, rather than using donation sites as a glorified trash can.

2. **Resell** For nice and clean unwanted clothes, why not make some money by selling them on eBay or Thredup.com?

3. **Clothing take-back** Many clothing and shoe businesses are trying to close the textile-waste loop by offering a clothing take-back credit at their stores. For example, at Patagonia retail locations, customers can trade in their used gear and obtain credit toward another new item. The same goes for *H&M* and Nike— usually they will accept any textiles, not just their own brand's garments. *Levi Strauss & Co* offers 20% off a new pair of jeans to customers who drop off a pair of denim at their *Levis* or Outlet store.

4. **Recycle** Some places have textile recycling where any old, worn-out clothes (underwear and socks included) can be discarded. You can find your nearest drop-off location at smartasn.org. Additionally, at RecycleNow.com you also can find the closest textile recycling bin. A wonderful company, Terracycle's whole business is to recycle and upcycle old stuff, so you can order a box for textile recycling from them. *Nike* and *H&M* also collect worn clothes for recycling.

5. **Blue Jeans Go Green** This program collects denim across the country and recycles the worn fabric into insulation. The Blue Jeans Go Green program keeps textile waste out of landfills and helps with building efforts in communities around the country.

Chapter 11
Zero Waste Laundry

"Use it up, Wear it out, Make it do, or Do without."

– Boyd K. Packer
American religious leader

Wash, fold, repeat. I feel like I'm always doing laundry (something I'm sure we all feel). Laundry is about clean clothes, yet it can be such a dirty task. Too many laundry detergents contain many chemicals and come in plastic. Did you know that 700 million laundry detergent jugs end up in either a landfill or an ocean each year? If you also add fabric softener, dryer sheets, and the dryer, the impact on the planet adds up.

Luckily, the green movement has taken hold in some very important areas of our domestic lives, which includes laundry, and there are ways to reduce waste and still have clean clothes.

Green Laundry Tips

1. **Wash your clothes less frequently**
   Spoiler alert: they'll last longer, too! The process of repetitive washing and drying weakens the fibers. With each wash, microfibers enter the water system and often are ingested by fish. University of California researchers discovered that on average, synthetic fleece jackets release 1.7 grams of microfibers with each wash. Two solutions are being investigated: (a.) a filter to be installed on washing machines, and (b.) the development of waterless appliances, whereby textiles are "washed" in pressurized carbon dioxide.

2. **Stop washing everything after a single use**
   Okay, certain items do need to be washed frequently — underwear, gym clothes, your husband's socks (especially those). But not everything needs to go into the

We invested in an Ikea drying rack that can be extended when in use and folded for easy storage.

hamper after one wear. Jeans are a great example: even denim manufacturers recommend that jeans be worn several times before laundering. Denim is meant to be extremely durable (think cowboys) and, after so many wears should begin forming to the shape of your body. Frequent washing causes the fabric to lose its form-fitting quality and to fade over time. Other garments that should be re-worn before washing include sweaters, jackets, sweatshirts, and pajamas.

3. Use cold water for the wash.

Most of your energy usage in the laundry process comes from heating the water. It is not necessary — or even beneficial — to wash everything in hot water. Heat is not very nice to your clothes — it causes dyes to bleed and breaks down the integrity of fabrics. Wash only one out of every five loads in hot water — but keep in mind that underwear and sheets should always be washed in hot water in order to kill bacteria.

4. Line dry or use a drying rack.

You can easily lower your energy consumption by using a drying rack during the cold seasons and a clothesline in the spring/summer. Aside from the environmental benefits, it is also better for your clothes. Agitation from the dryer is harsh on fabrics, and the heat can cause static cling. Air-drying your clothes allows the moisture to naturally dissipate and clothes to keep their shape longer. I've also heard from many people who line dry that the sun acts as bleach on their whites. One more laundry product you can eliminate!

5. **Wash complete loads.**

   This is pretty obvious. Washing only a half-load is a waste of water and electricity. Make sure you are loading your washer up to three-fourths full. A hundred years ago people had to hand wash their clothes in a tub, then lay each piece on a drying rack or hang them on a clothesline to dry. This process would consume hours of the day, which is unrealistic for the modern mom. While I don't think we should necessarily regress a hundred years, I do think we can take some tips from the past and return to a more natural way of cleaning clothes. Making these simple changes will be better for your clothes, wallet, and the planet.

6. **Ditch those commercial laundry products and opt for natural or homemade solutions.**

   Conventional laundry detergents leave a dirty mess and are potentially toxic to humans. Many of the chemicals used in common detergents and softeners pollute our water supply as well as leave a residue, which can lead to skin irritations and other health issues. The internet is a mecca for homemade detergent recipes. Just google "homemade detergent" and you'll get hundreds of websites and blogs with different recipes and reviews. Experiment with one until you find a keeper. An added bonus is that the main ingredients are so cheap that the average cost per load is around five cents (about 1/5 the cost of commercial brands). Personally, I use soap nuts which I talk about below. Chemical-free and zero-waste laundry detergent brands I like are True Earth, Dropps and Earth Breeze.

7. **Use reusable dryer balls instead of dryer sheets.**

   Dryer sheets contain chemicals that can break down fibers, so your clothes will last longer by switching to dryer balls. You can even add a few drops of essential oils like citrus or lavender to make your laundry smell nice. For top loaders, add a cup of white vinegar to your rinse cycle to clean and deodorize your clothes; it also acts as a natural fabric softener.

Soap nuts – which are actually berries from a bush – are a great alternative to laundry soap.
They're inexpensive, 100 % natural, contain no chemicals, and biodegradable.

Soap Nuts

Soap nuts are actually a berry from a bush and are naturally rich in saponins, which
are a pure cleaning solution. They are free of perfume, chemicals, hypo-allergenic, and
odorless. The bushes are easy-to-grow, organic, and require very little packaging. For
one wash, use about five nuts in a reusable bag. The nuts can be used over and over
again for many washes until they get mushy and gray — at which point they can be
composted in your garden. At first I had my doubts that they would work on dirty cloth
diapers, but I was happily surprised to discover that they clean like any commercial
laundry detergent filled with chemicals. Since a package of soap nuts lasts practically
forever, it will also save you some real money. If you still want some fragrance, try
adding a few essential oil drops (such as lavender or lemon) to the laundry.

Fabric Softener

20-30 drops of essential
oil, *(lavender, citrus and
rosemary are my favorites),*
to 1 gallon of white vinegar

Close lid and shake to mix together. When
it's laundry time, shake the bottle and use
⅓ cup per normal wash load. *Use half these
amounts for front loading washer.*

So maybe you're not completely nuts for soap nuts — no worries! Today there are plenty of companies making environmentally friendly laundry detergent. My favorite is *Dropps* because of its minimal packaging. *Dropps* also makes dishwasher tablets (which I also use). Other zero waste laundry brands are *Tru Earth* and *Earth Breeze*.

DIY Laundry Detergent and Stain Remover

Homemade laundry detergents are super easy to make and work just as well as the conventional ones. Added bonuses — they are less expensive and easy on the environment. Here are some of my favorites:

Basic Detergent

⅓-½ **Cup of Liquid Castile Soap,** for a large load in a top loader washer

During the rinse cycle, add ½ cup of vinegar. *Use half these amounts for front loading washer.*

Stain Remover

1 Cup Water
½ Cup Hydrogen Peroxide
½ Cup Baking Soda
¼ Cup Lemon Juice

Mix together and apply to stain. Store in a dark container for a least 20 minutes, (or over night). Then wash as usual. You can also pour the mixture, (minus the water), directly into the washing machine with your laundry soap and wash as usual.

Chapter 12

Zero Waste Packed Lunches

"You cannot get through a single day without having an impact on the world around you. What you do makes a difference, and you have to decide what kind of difference you want to make."

– Jane Goodall
Global community conservationist

Too many people have come to depend on convenient and individually wrapped items for school lunches. Of course it's way more time-saving and easy to pack lunch items in single-use plastic bags, aluminum foil, or wax paper, or even to purchase single-serving items in disposable packaging. The problem with these items is the huge environmental cost they represent — and landfills are already full to overflowing from convenient, individually wrapped foods. In addition, food packaging can contain harmful chemicals that can leach into the food or drink you consume.

Ok, so packing a zero waste and healthy lunch for kids might not be super convenient — but it's doable and does not take as much time as you might imagine. Steps you can take to lessen your lunch's carbon footprint include reusing containers and taking a thermos (see photo) for beverages and soup. I like plastic-free bento boxes from *Lunch Bots* and thermos soup containers for soup, burritos, and stews. I have reusable metal bottles for water and Mason jars with lids for iced tea. I also send the kids with reusable cutlery and cloth napkins. If I have to wrap food, I use either a cloth sandwich bag or beeswax wrap to ensure we're not ending up with unwanted waste. I also pack lunches in either a backpack or insulated bag that will keep things cool. Since we live in a warm climate, I also include ice packs.

Since reforming to a zero waste lifestyle, the bulk section and I have become good friends. I use cloth bags instead of plastic bags to bring home dried foods. I buy nuts, pretzels, and dried fruit this way — and I have even found yummy chia energy

To pack a zero waste lunch, we use a reusable bento box or thermal soup container, a metal water bottle, cutlery, and cloth napkin. For wrapped food, we use a cloth or beeswax wrap.

snacks for a sweet treat without loads of sugar to add to my kids' lunch boxes. Instead of buying snack packs wrapped in plastic, I buy a large pack of crackers and include a few in their lunches.

The food industry makes snacks convenient, but they usually come in plastic. Energy bars (like Larabars) are a great snack to pack in the kid's lunchbox. However, considering how much they cost, they are not very sustainable for either my wallet or the planet. The good news is that making your own is not very difficult. Here are my recipes.

Fruit Leather

Of all the kids' snacks you can buy, fruit leather must be the biggest rip-off because making your own is so super easy. Forget those processed, sugary fruit leathers, and say hello to juicy fruit leathers bursting with natural flavors — and containing only fruit. As a bonus, they are plastic-wrap free.

Basically, fruit leather is a snack made by pureeing and dehydrating fruits and berries. My kids absolutely love these snacks, and it's very easy for the kids to make, too. I like them because they are the perfect treat with no processed sugar. Once you make them, you can store them in an airtight container for a few weeks at least. They are small and light, so they are easy to bring along for a snack on the go or as a treat in a school lunch. I always make my fruit leathers in a dehydrator because this way I don't have to stay home and wait for them to be finished. But they also can be made in an oven in just a few hours.

There are many options for package-free and zero waste snacks for kids, like making your own from scratch or buying in bulk.

Here are some of my favorite flavor combinations, but be adventurous and try out all kinds of fun combinations, or just use a single fruit or berry. I have heard that adding beets makes them very colorful and even more nutritional.

DIY Fruit Leather

Combine fruit and/or berries in a blender or food processor and blend until completely pureed. Pour fruit onto a dehydration tray lined with a reusable liner or parchment paper. Dehydrate at 115 degrees for 8-12 hours until the puree is firm and can be peeled off. Slice or cut strips with a knife or scissors. Roll up and store in a bag or airtight container.

Banana and Raspberry

2 ripe bananas

1 cup raspberries

Blueberry and Banana

2 ripe bananas

1 cup ripe blueberries

Blueberry and Mint

2 cups blueberries

1 tbsp maple syrup

1 drop of peppermint essential oil

Cinnamon Apple

2 cups unsweetened apple sauce

2 tsp ground cinnamon

You can use almost any fresh or dried fruit to make fruit leathers. Some of our favorite and simplest — just puree the fruit and dry into leathers.

Peaches

Use ripe, fresh peaches. You can leave the peels on

Strawberries

Use sweet and ripe strawberries

Apricots

Soak dried apricots for a few hours to soften them before pureeing

Crackers

2 cups white spelt flour or all-purpose flour

2 tsp baking powder

1 tsp baking soda

1 tbsp sugar

6 tbsp cold butter (I used Earth Balance butter)

2 tsp olive oil

2/3 cup water

3 tbsp melted butter

1 tsp salt

Preheat oven to 400 F.

Add the flour, baking powder, baking soda, sugar in a food processor and pulse to combine. Add the cold butter in pieces and mix to combine. Add olive oil and then water, little at the time until you have a dough ball.

Roll out dough as thin as possible with a rolling pin on a flat surface, dusted with flour to avoid sticking. Cut out crackers with a cookie cutter (we used a round one and one heart shaped one). Place crackers on parchment papers on a cookie sheet and bake for 10 minutes. Flip all crackers and bake until slightly golden.

Remove crackers from oven and brush them with melted butter and sprinkle salt over. Leave until cool.

Use beeswax wraps instead of plastic or zip lock bags to wrap sandwiches or half of an avocado.

Homemade "Lärabars"

1 cup unsalted cashews or almonds
1 cup pitted dates
½ tsp of vanilla extract
1 small pinch salt
Flavor option:
2 tsp cocoa powder or
1 tsp pumpkin spice or
2 tsp spirulina

Blend in a food processor until it is a sticky dough. Form into any shape and place on parchment paper. I personally like to make them look like Lära Bars. Freeze for a couple of hours. Keep in fridge to keep them fresh for a month.

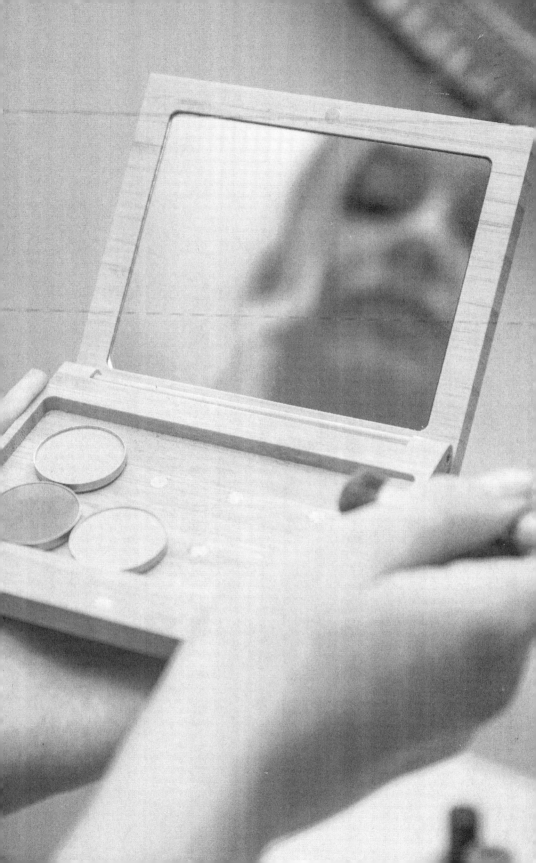

Chapter 13
Zero Waste Body Care

*"We have not come here to beg the world leaders to care.
We have come to let them know change is coming."*

– Greta Thunberg
Swedish environmental activist

L et's be honest—the bathroom can be the trickiest place to go green. Going zero waste means reducing both waste as well as chemicals — especially when it comes to beauty routines. Of course, eco-friendly shampoos, conditioners, moisturizers, and makeup are available. However, even though these products are considered "green," if they're still in disposable packaging, it defeats the purpose. Going zero waste means forgoing not only disposable items, but also their packaging.

Changing your makeup to a zero waste routine makes the biggest difference! Of course, one option is to stop wearing makeup altogether, but for me that is a step too far. Just because I'm considered a "granola mom" doesn't mean I don't like wearing makeup. That being said, think about all the plastic in our makeup bags right now, then imagine all the trash created over the years — as each supply of makeup item runs out shortly after purchase.

If you're ready to ditch the plastic for good, try creating makeup at home with some of these ideas:

- **Makeup Removal** Forget old-fashioned makeup remover in bottles and wipes; instead, say hello to super easy DIY makeup remover. First, you can try the old trick of a washcloth with water and some bulk soap. If that does not work, you can use homemade makeup remover pads.

- **Moisturizer** Coconut oil is a wonderful light and natural moisturizer, as is shea butter. Be sure to find organic, unrefined, and fair-trade products in glass jars so that you can reuse and refill them. Coconut oil can be applied to wet skin before drying off to help seal in moisture. Keep a jar by your bath.

Makeup Remover

4-ounce jar

small cloth wipes, (*I use cloth wipes that I cut from old towels*)

1½ - 2 tbsp of fractionated coconut oil

1 tsp of castile soap

½ cup witch hazel

2 - 4 drops of essential oils (*lavender, lemon or frankincense are great essential oils to use on your skin*)

1. Place cotton pads in a glass jar.
2. In a small bowl, mix the coconut oil and the castile soap.
3. Pour mixture over cotton pads. Press down on the pads so the soap and coconut oil evenly absorb into them.
4. Pour just enough witch hazel over pads to wet them.
5. Place the lid on the jar and shake, (*this helps to evenly distribute over the pads*).

- **Oatmeal Face Mask** Oats are great for your body — both inside and out. Oats contain anti-inflammatory properties, so it's great for anyone suffering from acne and can help calm itchy and irritated skin. Oats contain a property called beta-glucan that can form a fine film on the skin, helping to clean it and providing a deep moisturizer.

- **DIY Lotion Bars** I make lotion bars to keep my skin soft. Lotion bars also make natural personal gifts for all occasions. You can make them unscented or add essential oils for nice smells or even add dried flowers to make them really pretty. Shaped like a heart, they are well suited for Valentine's Day. A flower mold is ideal on Mother's Day. Not only does making your own lotion bars save you money, but they are also easy to pop into your purse, and they are easier to use than bottled lotions.

Oatmeal Face Mask

1 tbsp ground oatmeal
½ ripe banana
1 tbsp plain yogurt

1. Use the back of a fork to mash and blend everything into a paste.
2. Apply to face and neck, and leave on for 15 minutes.
3. Remove with warm water or a warm wet washcloth.

Not only does making your own lotion bars save you money, but they are also easy to pop into your purse and easier to use than bottled lotions.

DIY Lotion Bars

6 tbsp cocoa butter

1 tbsp of shea butter

1 tbsp of almond oil

1 tsp vitamin E oil (optional)

5 drops of essential oil,
(like Joy, lavender, citrus or chamomile, optional)

Combine all ingredients (except essential oils if using) in a double boiler or a glass bowl over a smaller saucepan with 1 inch of water in it. For a low maintenance approach, combine ingredients in a quart-size glass mason jar, then place jar into a small saucepan of water until melted. Turn the burner on and bring water to a boil. Stir ingredients constantly until they are melted and smooth. Remove from heat, let cool a bit, then add any desired essential oils and/vitamin E. Gently stir by hand until the essential oils are incorporated. Carefully pour into molds or whatever you will be allowing the lotion bars to harden in. I used silicone baking cups for easy removal, though any mold would work. Allow the lotion bars to cool completely before attempting to pop them out of the molds.

Watch out for endocrine disruptors!

Endocrine disruptors are chemicals (some are natural and others are synthetic) that harm our body's endocrine systems. They have been linked to early puberty immune dysfunction, certain cancers, respiratory problems diabetes, obesity, cardiovascular problems, and learning disabilities.

Switch to natural, fragrance free and paraben-free beauty products – Shampoo conditioner, deodorants, (or make your own), moisturizer, cosmetics, perfume, soaps, and even toothpaste and other personal care products often contain endocrine disruptors.

If you're not up for the mess of making your own makeup but don't want to support big beauty businesses, then consider buying makeup made by hand by the many sellers on Etsy.com. I have found some really good makeup there. I do purchase makeup from different sources, too.

Here are my favorite Zero Waste and chemical-free makeup brands

- **Antonym Cosmetics** Not all of their makeup is zero waste, but lots of it is packed in bamboo containers, and all of it is cruelty free and vegan (credobeauty.com).
- **Elate Cosmetics** This is my personal favorite. Not only are they toxin free, cruelty free, vegan, and packed in bamboo containers — but they also offer refills (elatebeauty.com).
- **Glow Organic** This brand is natural and uses organic ingredients. They also use recycled, recyclable, and biodegradable materials for their packaging and displays (gloworganicbrighton.co.uk).
- **Aether Beauty** Are organic, fair-trade, vegan, and non-GMO ingredients wherever possible. Their eyeshadow palette is completely paper and the packaging is almost entirely recyclable (Āthr Beauty) .
- **RMS** Uses organic and toxic-free ingredients and some of their products come in recycled glass pots, and their boxes are made from 80% post-consumer recycled fiber and manufactured using 100% wind power. (rmsbeauty.com)
- **Axiology** Their lipstick tubes are made from recyclable aluminum. Their packaging is made from recycled trash and is both recyclable and compostable. Everything is certified vegan and cruelty-free and is completely free of palm oil, gluten, soy, and synthetic fragrances. (axiologybeauty.com)

Refillable makeup or plastic-free cosmetics are becoming more popular – probably by consumer demand – so now there are some good options.

Body Care

- **Shaving** I simply use a reusable metal shaver and soap.
- **Nails** I use a stainless-steel nail clipper and file and a few drops of oil for healthy cuticles.
- **Perfume** Perfume is filled with toxins that seep into the skin and eventually into the bloodstream and are also inhaled into the lungs when you give yourself a spritz. But it is a tough area to do zero waste because there are no bulk options – that I'm aware of, at least. You could choose nontoxic perfumes; although I simply decided to nix them altogether for a few drops of essential oils mixed with a little oil instead. My favorite essential oils for perfume are Joy, citrus fresh, and lavender from Young Living.
- **Deodorant** It's been many years since I stopped buying deodorant and started making my own. It's so easy and works like a charm. The best part is that I make it with ingredients found in the kitchen — coconut oil, baking soda, and arrowroot — so it also saves me lots of money. The majority of store-bought deodorants contain chemicals like aluminum, paraben, and propylene — which are harmful to the body and the planet. Plus, they always come in plastic packaging.

Hair Care

One problem with store-bought hair products is that most of them come in plastic, which is a big no-no when trying to live zero waste. Another problem is that most

Safety razors are a great zero waste alternative to disposable razors.

commercial shampoos, conditioners, and styling products contain lots of harmful chemicals. I have adopted a different but still zero waste (or at least fairly zero waste) hair routine. Here it is:

- **Shampoo & conditioner** Most of the time, I buy my shampoo and conditioner in bulk at my local co-op and implement reusable bottles for them. Sometimes I'm lucky that my hair stylist and friend finds me shampoo without nasty chemicals and in post-recycled bottles. Yay!!!

Deodorant

⅓ cup coconut oil
10 drops of lavender essential oil
2 tbsp baking soda
1 tbsp arrowroot

Mix it all in a bowl, then put into a mason jar.

- **Hair Shine** Because I have curls, sometimes I need something to "tame" my wild hair and make it look shiny so I don't end up looking like a troll…a cute troll, but still a troll — so I use coconut oil. It's inexpensive, contains no chemicals, and a little goes a long way.
- **Brush and Comb** I use a brush and comb made from natural bamboo.
- **Moisturizing Hair Mask** If my hair feels tired and dry, I create a hair mask by making a paste. I use 3 heaping Tbsp. of Aztec Secret Healing Clay and 1 Tbsp. coconut oil; I add warm water and whisk it until it becomes a spreadable paste. I massage it into my hair and scalp, and leave it on for 20 minutes or so. After that, I wash it out with shampoo and then use a conditioner.
- **Hair Ties** They're bad for the environment for so many reasons: they are made of synthetic materials that contain chemicals, they are sold in plastic packaging, they don't last very long, and they become rubbish as soon as they break. The problem is that if you're like me and have lots of hair and sometimes need a quick hairdo in the morning, hair ties might seem like a necessity. I really like KOOSHOO and the Plastic-Free Organic Cotton Hair Ties from Life Without Plastic. They are made with organic cotton and rubber and sold in 100% recycled and/or biodegradable packaging.

Zero Waste Oral Care —Something To Smile About

When trying to avoid chemicals, we typically think of household cleaners, body products, and children's toys — but few of us ever pay attention to the chemicals we put into our mouths when brushing our teeth. Good oral hygiene is essential for a healthy mouth, confident smile, and fresh breath. However, most products on the market contain harsh chemicals, additives, detergents, dyes, and even sweeteners. Not to mention, most commercial dental products are made from various forms of plastic and come in wasteful packaging that's hard to recycle. Fortunately, there are natural and eco-friendly dental care alternatives out there— so let's talk about how to keep your smile shining without unnecessary waste and harmful chemicals.

- **Toothbrushes** Try to imagine how many toothbrushes you've used in your life (probably several each year)! Each time you're finished with a plastic toothbrush, you most likely throw it into the trash. Consider all the toothbrushes you and your family have thrown away over the years! That's a huge contribution to our ever-growing plastic problem that continues to burden Mother Earth. A great natural alternative to plastic toothbrushes are bamboo ones. They are the most environmentally-conscious toothbrushes on the market as bamboo is a sustainable raw material. It can grow up to four inches per day with little water and does not require pesticides or fertilizer. Another bonus is that bamboo is naturally resistant to many types of bacteria—which makes your toothbrush last much longer (and keeps your mouth healthier)!

- **Toothpaste** Most popular commercial toothpastes contain harsh chemicals, additives, detergents, dyes, and sweeteners — which can be harmful to your teeth, overall health, and the environment. Certain ingredients such as triclosan and fluoride found in toothpaste can bioaccumulate in the environment, affecting ecosystems and harming wildlife. Although you spit out most of the toothpaste, chemicals still find their way into your bloodstream because your mouth is one of the most absorbent parts of your body.

- **Chemicals found in popular toothpastes**
  - Triclosan — Hormone-disrupting chemical
  - Sodium Lauryl Sulfate (SLS) — An additive that allows products to foam and has been linked to cancer, neurotoxicity, organ toxicity, skin irritation, and endocrine disruption.
  - Diethanolamine (DEA) — Linked to cancer
  - Microbeads — These beads of plastic not only contain hormone disruptors, but also cause lots of problems in water and oceans.
  - Titanium Dioxide (TiO2) — Carcinogenic and linked to cancer
  - Parabens — Contain hormone-disrupting chemicals and have been linked to infertility, thyroid issues, and cancer.

The good news is that there are many different options for chemical-free toothpastes on the market — but since they still come in plastic, I personally use toothpaste tablets or toothpaste powder (which is zero waste). I buy my toothpaste tablets from my local zero waste store so I can buy them package-free. However, you can also buy them at Target, Whole Foods, health food stores, and online. Most of them come plastic-free in glass jars or paper bags. They're simple to use: for the tablets, just start chewing and then brush with a wet brush, or sprinkle the powder and then brush with a wet brush.

Another option for zero-waste toothpaste is making your own. Here's my recipe:

DIY zero-waste toothpaste
1/2 cup bentonite clay powder (food grade)
1/8 tsp. unrefined high-mineral salt
2 tsp. baking soda
2/3 cup water (more if paste is too thick)
1/4 cup coconut oil
1 tsp. Stevia (optional)
1-4 drops of essential oil (options listed below)

There are so many package – free and zero waste personal care options available these days – from shampoo and soap, to toothbrushes, toothpaste, and razors.

- **Essential oils for oral care**

  Cinnamon — Contains antifungal and antibacterial properties

  Spearmint oil — A strong antiseptic that eliminates germs and helps heal wounds

  Thieves oil — Good for gingivitis, helps with bad breath, kills bacteria, and reduces swelling of inflamed gums

  Mix everything until you have a paste. Add more water if it seems too dry. You can keep this toothpaste in an airtight mason jar.

- **Dental Floss** Yes, even dental floss can harm us and our planet. Many floss products are made from nylon — a synthetic fiber derived from petroleum products. Nylon takes nearly fifty years to break down in earth's natural environment. Most floss is coated in a petroleum-based wax that can pollute water sources and harm wildlife. Petroleum is a non-sustainable resource that impacts soil, ground, water, and ecosystems. Considering that Americans buy over three million miles of dental floss every year, that's a lot of plastic waste. A much better option is to invest in a refillable container and simply refill it with dental floss made from natural and compostable material like natural mulberry silk. I buy mine at my local co-op, but it can also be found at lifewithoutplastic.com. This floss is coated in plant-based material and natural wax—making it 100% biodegradable, so you can throw the floss into a compost after using it.

- **Mouthwash** While there's a label on most name-brand mouthwashes warning the consumer not to drink the mouthwash, we unknowingly ingest many chemicals while simply rinsing. Some of these chemicals include thymol, eucalyptol, hexetidine, methyl salicylate, benzalkonium chloride, cetylpyridinium chloride, methyl paraben, hydrogen peroxide, and alcohol. These chemicals have been known to cause health problems related to respiratory, nervous, reproductive, and neural systems. And the list goes on: unstable heartbeats, muscle pain, plaque buildup, breast tumors — even death. To switch up your mouthwash regimen, look for a mouthwash that uses essential oils like peppermint, witch hazel, cinnamon, spearmint, or thieves — or make your own zero-waste mouthwash with this recipe:
  - 1 cup alcohol-free witch hazel
  - 4 drops Thieves essential oil
  - 2 tsp baking soda

  Mix ingredients in a dark container and store in a cool, dark place. Shake well before using.

- **Oil Pulling** To easily amp up your oral care routine, consider oil pulling! Simply swish one tablespoon of coconut oil in your mouth for 15-20 minutes to get rid of the harmful bacteria in your mouth. The way it works is simple: when you swish the oil around your mouth, the bacteria gets stuck in the oil and then dissolves in the liquid oil. Oil pulling studies have shown a reduction in harmful bacteria, plaque, gingivitis, and bad breath. Don't forget to brush your teeth once you are finished!

- **Zero Waste Periods** An average woman will use around 16,000 or more tampons or pads during her lifetime. That's 7 billion tampons and pads landing in landfills each year. Most of them contain chemicals, toxins, additives, and synthetic materials such as plastic. The plastics, first of all, take a very long time to break down. Second, they also end up leaking into nature, thereby polluting our rivers, lakes, streams, and world.
  So here are the better zero waste options:

  ### Menstrual Cup
  The first green menstrual products you'll probably want to check out are menstrual cups. Designed to replace tampons, they're usually made from medical grade silicone. Although some companies say to replace them every year or two, most people get 5-10 years out of them over a lifetime, which equals 4-8 cups vs. thousands of tampons. It really does make a big difference for Earth!

Cloth Pads

Reusable sanitary pads are very similar to disposables, except that they're made with cloth, bamboo, charcoal, and other natural materials. As with menstrual cups, they can last 5–10 years, and a single pad potentially can replace thousands of disposables.

The major negative is that you have to wash them. However, if you don't care about staining, just throw them in with your regular laundry: it really is that easy. If you do care about staining, soak them in cold water after use. I wash mine with soap nuts and line dry them in the sun, which naturally bleaches and disinfects them. I use pads, which I bought from Life Without Plastic.

Period Underwear

These are my daughter's favorite because period underwear look and feel almost identical to regular underwear but can absorb several tampons' worth of blood, depending on the style you choose. Organic cotton and other sustainable fabrics can offer better breathability. There are many brands, but we like Everie and Bamboo.

Plastic-Free Pads and Tampons

If reusable just seems like too much of a challenge, there are also plastic-free pads and tampons. The plastic-free options usually are organic as well, and they have a number of advantages over conventional pads and tampons.

Although organic pads and tampons are a bit more expensive, many people find that they're worth it for the advantages listed above.

Ready to Make the Switch?

Beyond being better for the environment, green period products are better for your health. And, in the case of menstrual cups and reusable pads, they will save you a ton of money. I made the switch over 10 years ago. Now I have a teenage daughter using reusable products, so I estimate that we have saved over $2000 so far.

Chapter 14
Zero Waste Picnics

"Let me make this simple — food waste that goes to the landfill creates methane gas which is pure poison, while food that ends up in a compost becomes pure nutrients for the planet."

— Fredrika Syren, *Activist, environmental writer, mom*

There is nothing my kids like more than an outdoor picnic. We'll bring a blanket and picnic lunch to enjoy on the grass after any outdoor activities. It's funny how a meal outdoors on a blanket somehow just tastes better. I like this option better than grabbing lunch at a restaurant because a picnic lunch is healthier and cheaper for a family of five.

However, a traditional picnic can create lots of waste — everything from leftover food, plastic cups and utensils, to paper napkins and plates. The good news is that it's possible to organize a zero waste picnic. Here's how to make sure your picnic is as green as the grass that you will be dining on:

1. **Invest in a picnic basket.**

   Let's begin with how you transport the food. Forget wasteful disposable plastic or paper bags and invest in a cooler or a picnic basket made with natural material like bamboo or natural willow. A backpack or a reusable shopping bag can work as well.

2. **Skip the disposable items.**

   Invest in reusable bamboo or plant-based plates and cups as well as utensils, and use cloth napkins. If you do need to bring disposable plates, etc., then make sure they are made from either corn or potato starch. We always bring a compostable plastic bag to gather food scraps that we'll either bring to our compost or to a commercial composting facility. We bring the food that

Picnics are such fun! And an affordable family activity that is so easy to do with little or no waste.

we're going to eat in reusable zip lock bags or in reusable food containers. Skip the juice boxes because, not only do they generate lots of trash, but they also contain lots of sugar. A green and healthy tip is to put flavored water or homemade vitamin water or lemonade in reusable stainless steel water bottles with reusable straws for the kids.

Here is how you make vitamin water:

- Use a wide mouth glass canning jar of just about any size. Either a quart or pint size is easy to have ready and waiting in the fridge or carry with you, or use a glass pitcher.

- Fill the container ¼ to ½ full with a combination of chopped fruit and/or herbs (organic is ideal for this). Then fill the container to the top with water, cover, and leave in the refrigerator for at least 2-3 hours, or up to a full day to infuse.

- When you're thirsty, strain out the fruit and herbs and enjoy the fresh flavored drink. Most of the time, I strain the infused water from the fruit once and refill the jar or pitcher for one more infusion.

3. **Make the menu organic and sustainable.**

   I love going to our local organic farmers market to pick up a lunch that we'll enjoy in nature together because fresh and local food is my favorite food to eat. But you don't have to go to a farmer's market to find sustainable food. Just choose seasonal, organic, and local food at your local grocery store for your picnic.

4. **Don't overpack food.**

   The problem with packing too much food is that it might spoil because you do not have a way to keep it cold.

5. **Compost.**

   Remember to compost your scraps and wine/champagne cork. We always bring a container or large Mason jar to gather food scraps that we'll either bring to our compost.

6. **Pick up after yourself.**

   Make sure to gather your belongings before you leave. Don't leave any food scraps as they might be compostable but not good for wildlife to eat. My general rule is to leave things better than when we arrived.

Chapter 15

Zero Waste
Takeout

"The earth is what we all have in common."

— Wendell Berry, *American*
novelist, environmental activist

Takeout food is a guilty pleasure that we all enjoy from time to time, but here's where the "guilty" part comes in— all that waste. Takeout food comes in Styrofoam or plastic containers (even most cardboard containers are non-recyclable due to the thin plastic moisture lining on the interior), plastic forks and knives in their own plastic wrappers, disposable chopsticks, plastic lids, plastic straws, tinfoil or paper wrappers, condiment packets, sauce tubs, a stack of paper napkins, takeout menus/coupons/printed receipts, brown paper bags, and a plastic bag to carry it all in.

It's depressing, difficult, and nearly impossible to recycle. But with a little extra planning, you can still enjoy takeout food minus the waste by bringing your own containers to the restaurant.

Takeout Tips:

- When placing your order, call and ask if you can use your own containers.
- Always be polite and smile — compliment their food.
- Thank the waitstaff profusely for accommodating your request.
- Bring spotlessly CLEAN containers with tight-fitting lids.
- Include a generous tip (20% goes a long way).
- Walk or bike to and from the restaurant, if possible.
- Coffee shops and juice bars are well-accustomed to filling personal containers.
- A set of tiffins (stackable containers) is easy to transport and keeps different foods separated.
- Mason jars are great for soups, smoothies, sauces, and other liquids.

Chapter 16

Zero Waste Gifts

"The most environmental product is the one you didn't buy."

— Joshua Becker,
American author, minimalist

T he National Retail Federation's annual survey of holiday spending estimates that the typical American spent $659 on gifts for family, friends, and co-workers in 2019.

In my opinion, the perfect gift is one that can be appreciated as a long-term keepsake and has rich personal meaning. Let's face it: gift giving isn't easy, especially in our world of mass production, where many gifts no longer have a unique value to them. Why give the stereotypical gift from a department store when you can find a treasured piece of art, repurpose something old, or create something completely new? Creating zero waste keepsakes or finding eco-friendly natural gifts might require a DIY attitude, but it's doable and worth it.

Here are some environmental-friendly gift-giving tips that won't break the bank

1. Buy Used

Check out thrift stores. Books, in particular, are popular gifts — and many used books from bookstores are still in mint condition. See what's available on websites such as *Craigslist* where you'll often find items priced as "best offer" from people who may just want to declutter and are willing to negotiate. In all these cases, you will be eliminating excess packaging.

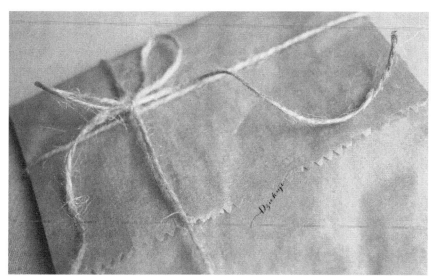

Brown paper bags and paper shopping bags makes great wrapping paper for gifts.

2. **Buy in bulk**

   From a bulk food store or special area in your supermarket, select nuts, dried fruits, candy, or other holiday treats. Some bulk stores will weigh empty jars prior to filling them and even offer a discount for using your own containers.

3. **DIY gifts**

   Individuals with access to a kitchen, sewing machine, workshop, fabrics, wool, art and craft supplies, paints, paper, computer or a camera can design gifts that are simple and inexpensive.

4. **Give an experience**

   In my opinion, time is priceless and the most valuable gift of all. Treat your family to fun experiences like going to the beach, an amusement park, or going on a trip together.

5. **Buy less and donate instead**

   I think it's very nice to give a gift that can help others instead of worrying about buying the perfect gift for someone. Now, if this donation also helps save the planet, that's a win-win in my book. Some of my favorite charities that work toward making the planet better are The Environmental Defense Fund, Rainforest Action Network, and Beyond Pesticides (beyondpesticides.org).

Cloth gift bags or using cloth to wrap gifts works great; since they are reusable they can be used for many more gifts.

6. Wrapping

Instead of grabbing the most convenient gift wrap from the store, start thinking about how you can sustainably wrap your gifts. Give trees a fighting chance — don't doom them to twenty-seconds of stardom as they are eyed by the gift recipient, then almost instantly shredded to pieces and left to be scooped into a trash bag.

Fabric

Fabric is very much like wrapping paper, but I find it even easier to work with! The flexible fibers in the fabric make tying or knotting easier, and eliminates the need for tape! Gift recipients can get very crafty with their fabric wrapping and use it as a scarf, a bandana, a decorative piece, a napkin or their next gift wrapping! There are so many ways to gift wrap with fabric.

Beach Towels

Instead of simply gifting a beach towel, use it as the wrapping! Beach towels are best for your larger gifts, and can be thoughtfully tied with a jump rope! Perfect for a day of fun in the sun!

It used to be a rule of etiquette that says we shouldn't give people used gifts, but those days are gone. These days secondhand shopping is fashionable and good for the planet. Giving secondhand finds is a great affordable way to give one-of-a-kind homewares, electronics, children's toys, shoes, and clothing.

If you are going to buy new gifts, make sure they have as little impact on the planet as possible by only buying high-quality, ethical, organic, plastic-free, gifts.

BUY ETHICAL

BUY SECONHAND

Homemade gifts are always appreciated. Even if you are not good at woodworking, sewing, or knitting, there are other homemade gifts like cookie mixes, candles, frames, bath salts, and more.

DIY

Whether it is a trip to a place like the beach, a coffee date, spa date, or going for an ice cream, being with loved ones will do the trick and create fun memories more than a physical gift.

GIVE EXPERIENCE

© 2020 ZeroWasteFamily.com

DONATE

Donate money to charity as a gift. It's very nice to give a Christmas gift that can help others instead of worrying about buying the perfect gift for someone. Now, if this donation also helps save the planet, it's a win-win in my book.

Mason Jars

Mason Jars are a simple, inexpensive way of wrapping gifts! Put your gift inside the Mason jar and finish it off with an oversized ribbon tied around the glass to keep your recipients wondering what's inside.

Planting Pots

Clay planting pots are inexpensive and easy to decorate with paint or a permanent marker. Instead of a card, write your personal message directly on the pot. Then, whenever the recipient grows something in that pot, they will read the personal message you wrote and think of you.

Reusable Bags

Thankfully, totes are becoming the new fad and can be used just about anywhere you go. Most grocery stores offer their reusable bags for a very reasonable price. In fact, a reusable bag is probably cheaper than many of the gift bags found in your local store. The reusable bag is gift wrapping that keeps giving and giving! Just think about how often you use yours! Make it pretty by tying a big ribbon around the middle or tying the handles together!

Brown Paper Bag

If you're looking for an extremely inexpensive but crafty way to wrap, use your brown paper bags from the grocery store. They lend a gift that rustic feel and can be dressed up by adding something natural like a leaf or feather tied to the handle.

Newspaper/Butcher Paper

Very inexpensive and easy to use! Add a delicate ribbon or some dainty twigs to give your gift that extra something!

Chapter 17

Zero Waste School Supplies

"Being green is more than just buying 'eco'. It is an unshakable commitment to a sustainable lifestyle."

– Jennifer Nini, *Activist, @ecowarriorprincess*

Trying to live zero waste with school-age children can be tricky, but my motto is *find what I have at home already, borrow, buy used — and, as a last resort, buy quality and eco-friendly if I must*. I first check out *Craig's List, eBay*, or even thrift shops for used school supplies.

Backpacks Get a good–quality backpack that will last so you don't have to buy a new one every school year. Look for a backpack with a lifetime warranty (like Jansport backpacks), so if it breaks or falls apart, the company will fix it. You can also find secondhand backpacks — and thankfully, companies will often still honor the warranty attached to them. My kids all have backpacks from Fjällräven which is a sustainable brand and high quality.

Binders Cardboard with a center with screws, so when it falls apart you can remove the center and recycle the cardboard. You can then reuse the center with your own homemade cover or buy a replacement from the manufacturer. Many times, people have lots of binders lying around the house, so ask around if anyone has a used one you can have.

Folders Buy paper or cardboard, but avoid the plastic kind so that when they break, you can recycle the paper.

Many companies now sell a wide range of school and office supplies using recycled, natural, and post-consumer materials.

Pens and pencils Fountain pens are refillable, and there are lots of options for pencils made with recycled material. My favorites are Onyx and Green ballpoint pens and plantable pencils from Sprout.

Rulers Buy a durable stainless steel ruler or a wood ruler, not plastic.

Calculators This is best to buy used on eBay or Craig's list.

Lunch boxes Invest in a reusable bento box or thermal soup containers, as well as reusable metal bottles, reusable cutlery, and cloth napkins. If you have to wrap food, use either a cloth sandwich bag or beeswax wrap to ensure avoiding unwanted waste. See our chapter on Zero waste Packed Lunches for more info.

Print paper Buy only 100% recycled paper or FSC certified paper — and make sure it's not bleached.

Notebooks Buy a durable notebook made with 100% post-consumer recycled paper.

Books Try to borrow, buy used, or download books before buying new ones.

And last but not least, be sure to recycle all used papers from printers and notebooks as well as covers from binders and folders.

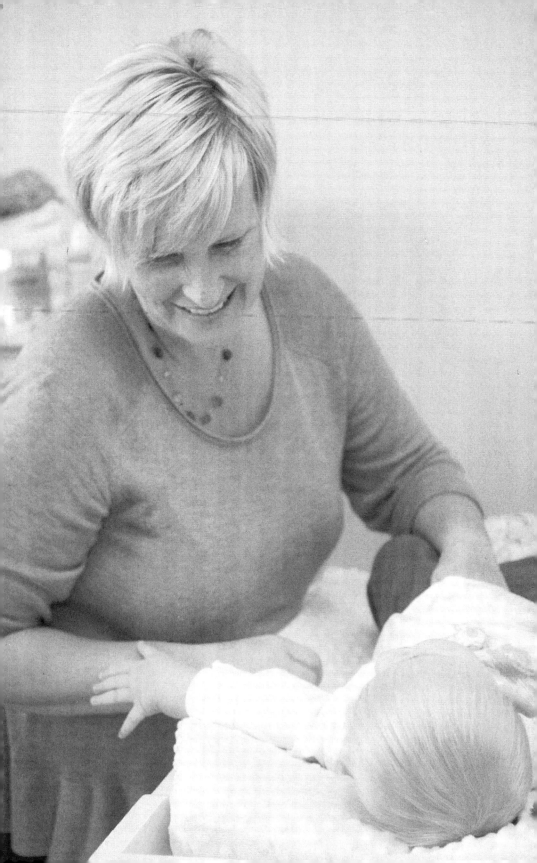

Chapter 18

Zero Waste Baby & Kids

"Start taking small steps for a healthier planet - there is zero time to waste!"

– Fredrika Syren, *Activist, environmental writer, mom*

W hen I had my first baby, I was shocked by how much waste I was suddenly producing. Between the disposable diapers, wipes, baby creams, baby food jars and containers, paper towels, and — of course, let's never forget the endless number of tissues it takes to wipe all those runny noses — I was filling up my trash bin way too fast. But over the years and three kids later, I learned piece by piece how to reduce disposable items and trade them in for more sustainable and eco-friendly items instead.

Let's begin with a major one— diapers!

Disposable diapers are simply bad for the planet: it's estimated that a child uses about 5,000 diapers during the baby years, so you can imagine how many diapers are filling up landfills all around the world! It takes 250-500 years for these diapers to break down. Single-use diapers are the third-largest waste item in landfills, with over 92% of them ending up in these dumping grounds.

The better option is to use cloth diapers because they are reusable and therefore clearly better for the environment. You won't be generating extra garbage for the collectors to pick up, and most medical experts agree that the toxin-free materials in cloth diapers prevent rashes and other issues like toxic shock syndrome. A wide variety of colorful and stylish options such as "All-in-Ones" (easy like disposables), "All-in-Twos" (cover and pad separates), waterproof diaper covers, inserts, and soakers are available now. Velcro makes them easy and safe to fasten. You can find a great comparison guide at thenaturalbabyco.com .

Let's face it, cloth diapers are reusable and, therefore, clearly better for the environment.

After taking the leap to cloth diapers, cloth wipes are the next natural progression. We use OsoCozy cloth wipes. They're super soft, reusable, and one less thing for the waste bin.

Bottles

Simply put, use baby bottles made from glass. Not only does a glass bottle last longer (unless you drop it, of course), but bottles made from glass pose no health problems. Neither hot nor warm liquids cause the glass material to break down (as plastics do). Plastic does not last as long as glass, which also can be recycled once it's no longer needed or breaks.

Managing Messes

With kids come messes, so paper towels come in handy. However, up to 51,000 trees are required to replace the number of paper towels that are discarded every day. Once used, paper towels cannot be recycled. Paper production is the fourth largest contributor to global climate change. On average, every American throws away 700 pounds of paper a year — resulting in 254 million tons of trash annually.

Instead, use cloth dish towels. You can usually find them at the grocery store, but at a steep markup. You can find them online for much cheaper—for example, I've found fifty flour-sack cloths for only $14.

Clothes

As most of us know, kids grow fast! So buying tons of brand new clothes not only gets expensive, but can also be wasteful. A great way to reduce waste is to buy used baby clothes or borrow them. I've never felt that all our baby stuff needed to be brand new; so, for our first child, almost everything was recycled, used, or borrowed from friends. Kids grow out of clothes so fast that there is no need to buy so much for them— especially babies. Of course, organic clothes are the best option for both your child and the planet though they can be very expensive, but these days there are many places to buy organic used baby clothes.

Unfortunately, organic clothes for both kids and adults may come with a hefty price tag; so how do you find affordable and safe clothing for your kids? First of all, my first baby had way more clothes than she ever needed, and as a matter of fact, many outfits were never worn because she grew so fast. With babies #2 and #3, I focused on a few great and versatile outfits, and bought them whenever there was a sale. I invested in only 7-10 outfits from the beginning. This allowed me to choose higher-quality options and not go bankrupt. I also found lots of great deals on used organic baby clothes sold on eBay and other sites. Now that my kids are older (9, 11, and 15), I still opt for organic clothing and buy most of it used.

I know that when it comes to keeping our babies safe, the number of hidden dangers can be overwhelming — it can be hard to know where to start. The basic idea is not trying to change the world on our own, but trying to do the best we can for our babies – or at least giving it an honest effort.

Green toys

As a mom of three who also wants to live an eco-friendly and chemical-free life, my rule of thumb is to avoid plastic toys at all costs. It's almost impossible to know which plastics are "safe" and which are not. Unfortunately, many toys are made from plastic due to its durability; and most plastic contains phthalates and/or Bisphenol-A (BPA) — both of which have been linked to cancer, hormone disruption, and developmental problems in children.

Lead is another chemical I worry about in toys. Many painted toys contain lead and other heavy metals, which have been linked to serious impairments in babies and children's developing brains. Yeah, you see the problem: toys may not be as innocent and safe as we parents would hope.

Buying toys and children's books at thrift stores, consignment shops, rummage sales, and online can be a great way to find good deals without breaking the bank.

Tips for buying safe toys

1. **Buy toys made with solid woods, wool, organic cotton, or stainless steel.**
   Toys painted with water-based or nontoxic paints are great, too.

2. **Favor non-battery-operated toys.**
   Not only are they better for the planet, but also, the batteries are loaded with toxins.

3. **Ask for used toys from friends and family.**
   My kids' favorite toys actually come from friends and family — when their

Kids never care if toys are previously owned; some of my kids favorite toys were previously owned – all they see is a toy.

kids outgrow the toys, they sell or gift them to us. My boys have a car track as well as wood blocks and legos that a friend traded me for homegrown vegetables from our garden. My boys absolutely love the toys, and I'm happy because rather than ending up in a landfill, the toys are being used more.

4. Favor high-quality toys.

As much as it pains me to say so, toys made with better and safer materials tend to be more expensive. The good news is that they also tend to last longer.

Nowadays, there are increasing numbers of healthy and chemical-safe toy brands available. The really good news is that what is a safe, toxic-free toy option for a child is also a much better alternative for the planet.

Here's a list of great Eco-friendly and Chemical-safe toy sellers:

Haba	North Star Toys
Green Toys	Tegu
Begin Again	Earth Hero
Toys	LieWood
Plan Toys	Cate and Levi
Wish Bone	Begin Again

Fredrika Syren

Chapter 19

Zero Waste and Raising Eco-minded Kids

"When life gives you compost, grow a garden."

– Farmer Bill, *City Farmers Nursery*

Talking to Your Kids About Climate Change

For a growing number of families all over the world, there's no avoiding it: climate change is already at their front door. My family lives in San Diego, but I grew up in Sweden. We see and feel the effects of climate change with droughts, low water levels, strange weather patterns, and lots of wildfires.

I think most kids know about climate change and struggle to deal with the constant barrage of anxiety-provoking news about the environment. And one of the biggest barriers is emotional. As an adult, I am worried about it – so imagine what it must be like for a child to deal with it. I firmly believe that avoiding talking about climate change and pretending it's not happening is far from the right answer.

So how do we talk to children about climate change?

According to an NPR/Ipsos poll, 84 % of parents in the USA, including a majority of both Democrats and Republicans, agreed that children should be learning about climate change. The polls also showed that only 45% of parents said they had talked to their own kids about it. A separate poll showed that 86% of teachers are even more supportive of teaching climate change in the classroom.

Experts agree that adults should talk to children about climate change, since it's important to help your children understand it and to support them as they cope with emotions. As a parent, I understand the wish to protect kids from scary facts about the planet they call home, but unfortunately, it won't make the problem go away; and they are more likely to hear it from someone else.

So how do you translate science-speak into kid-speak without overwhelming them — or even scaring them? Here are some ideas to break down climate change basics so you can empower your children to be part of the solution.

Check-In and listen

Check what they already know. According to Merav Segall, Licensed Marriage and Family Therapist (LMFT), start by finding out how much your child knows by asking "What do you know about climate change, and how do you feel about it? Most kids have more knowledge about climate change than we think, so the first step is to be a good listener. Depending on the age of the child you should approach it differently. For a younger child you might want to start by talking about earth and the importance of taking good care of it, while with older children you might want to talk about how carbon and trash affects the planet for example, Segall says.

Learn together

Learn about climate change together. My kids like watching documentaries like Kiss the Ground as well as reading books about climate change and learning together with us. As we learn, we also have open discussion about it and listen to what they think it means, researching more if things are confusing.

Listen

Listen to what your child's feelings are and what their fears are — This is so important for them to be heard and to be able to express their fears.

Give hope through knowledge

Give them hope and help them learn about the solutions. Kids need to not feel helpless, so you're giving them hope when they learn about the causes – and solutions – of climate change. Helping them establish a plan for personal action helps them feel they can do something, without glossing over the challenges that lay ahead. If we just give information, kids will feel powerless; so let them participate in solutions and actions, says Segall. Kids get anxious from the inability to act, and when feeling there is nothing they can do to help. So invite them to participate in family decisions that can help the planet, like bringing your own shopping bags, using reusable containers, buying an electric car, or starting a compost, Segall suggests. "I think my main message would be to give kids hope through action. That will look different at different ages".

This has been the part that has helped my kids the most. By having a plan for our personal efforts that they can also participate in, they feel more empowered.

The best things we can do to help our kids with their feelings about climate change is help turn their fear into action. This will help them feel they are part of the solution.

Of course, my kids know that our efforts alone can't save the planet, but that by starting conversations and inspiring everyone around us, more people will begin to make changes as well. This creates the ripples in the water that we need to make bigger changes.

Empower them to influence others

Finally, show children how influencing others — for instance, helping your kid ask a store manager to keep doors closed during summer to decrease the amount of CO_2 from the AC from escaping — is a giant step toward getting everyone to protect the Earth. Because, after all, that's really the best way we're going to solve this problem. Maybe see if as a family, you can start a recycling program at the school.

How to Raise Environmentally Conscious Kids

Teaching my kids about the value of the environment and the importance of preserving the world around them is an ongoing task. I feel it helps ensure a positive future for the earth. I'm raising three eco-minded kids: Isabella, 15; Noah, 11; and Liam, 9. I try to make our day-to-day routines ones that also teach them to care for the environment.

Gardening is a great way to teach kids about nature and the importance of trees, plants, water and sun, and how it all helps our planet.

Here is how I do it

Gardening Gardening and kids are a natural mix, involving dirt, digging, and water — children's favorites. Our garden is also a great classroom where my kids learn science, biology, and even math. We grow lots of vegetables and fruit. My children have learned how to plant a seed, which then sprouts, becoming a seedling that we then plant in our garden bed. They have learned that for the plant to grow, it needs water, compost, and sun. They also have learned how to provide these basics. Our children now understand how plants eat carbon and that plants also clean the air. They have learned how our bunny and chicken poop helps our garden. They have learned the important role of plants, bushes, and trees on our planet and how we simply can't cut down all trees and remove green patches without replacing them to conserve our planet.

Compost I believe it is important that we teach children to protect and restore the environment. Educating kids about composting is surely a great way to start. Composting truly is one of Mother Nature's most miraculous processes. Using only natural means to implement what is usually garbage, we're able to turn "waste" into one of the most beautiful and productive growing mediums available. Composting also teaches children how to reduce waste and keep it from going to a landfill. My kids now know that food waste in a landfill becomes methane gas, a potent greenhouse gas; whereas food waste in compost becomes powerful nutrients for our garden. A huge garden — or any garden at all — isn't necessary to have compost. As a matter of fact, composting can be done in an apartment.

Recycling Sorting through recycling is a surprisingly fun activity for my kids; even in nature or on the beach, they will pick up litter to recycle. It's also a good task to perform with kids so they learn what can and cannot go into a recycling bin. Recycling, just like composting, is a way to teach children how we can keep our waste from ending up in a landfill and how this can help save the planet. My kids even take it to the next level and will look in the recycle bins for materials for arts and crafts.

Spend time in nature There's no better way to connect with nature and help children appreciate our planet than getting outdoors. It's so great to see how almost anything — ants, worms, wildlife, mushrooms, flowers, funny-looking trees, puddles, and ice — can catch their attention forever. (I have an array of stones, twigs, leaves, and other items from nature that were just so special, they had to be saved.) Nature is a wonderful classroom where we can teach our children the importance of taking care of all the trees and water since they are homes for all the world's wonderful treasures. My children also like to write in their nature journals about what they see, feel. and experience when out and about, which gives them time to reflect and preserve memories.

If your children enjoy spending time outdoors, they'll more likely do everything they can to protect these green spaces and ensure they exist in the future.

Volunteer My family loves volunteering together, so we clean beaches with Surfride, collect food waste from our local farmers markets to give to families in need with Produce Good. Also, we cook dinner at the Ronald McDonald House. All these activities help my kids give back. The children learn how they can help strengthen our community, keep clean the beaches that provide so much fun, keep food waste out of landfills, and help those in need.

Be a good role model I know my kids watch us parents to see how we behave and react, so it's important that we be good role models. To this end, we show our kids how to be Earth-friendly by being Earth-friendly ourselves. Seeing our behavior will reinforce the importance of respecting our planet more than any verbal lesson.

Never in history has it been more important to encourage children to be green, to raise ecologically conscious children. I firmly believe I'm raising the next leaders for new innovations to care for our planet and make it livable for future generations.

Chapter 20

Zero Waste: Confessions of a Teenager

"Some people say that I should study to become a climate scientist so that I can "solve the climate crisis." But the climate crisis has already been solved. We already have all the facts and solutions. All we have to do is to wake up and change."

– Greta Thunberg,
Swedish environmental activist

I was nine years old when my family became zero waste, and before this zero waste journey, my dad was very stressed. He worked a lot and was not happy. He came home very late at night, so we did not see him very much. Since we became zero waste, my dad has been able to work less and spend more time with us, and he is so much happier. It makes me so happy, too.

At first I thought it was very challenging to live zero waste because I wanted so many things that were in plastic, and we were not supposed to buy things in plastic. But my mom and dad never make me or my brothers feel bad about if we want something that is not zero waste, but they do try to work with us to see if we can come up with a better alternative.

For example, my brothers like to build Legos, and my dad found you can buy them second hand. When we wanted roller-blades, bikes, skateboards, and surfboards, they bought them used but in great condition. My mom is great at finding the best clothes at thrift shops that are still cool and fashionable.

In the beginning, my friends and classmates were confused about the whole zero waste thing. When one of them came to my house and had some trash, I told them, "Sorry, we have no trash can, so feel free to take the trash with you." Or I will show

As a teenager, you can make small changes and inspire your family and friends to do the same. Be the change you wish to see in others.

them how to recycle or compost. Today, most of my friends are very supportive and even think it's cool. One of my best friends, who lives next door, her mom has started growing food, composting, and reducing plastic use because of our friendship. However, sometimes I do get those gotcha questions, and I have learned that I have to always answer any questions with lots of compassion and patience.

As a teenager you tend to live at home, which means you probably don't have the option of choosing; like in my case, I live zero waste because my parents made that decision, but you might personally want to reduce your family's waste stream, but maybe you have a family who is resistant. The good news is you can still make your own choices and reduce your own waste. Here are my tips.

Make your personal care waste free

Most teenagers do buy or request beauty products; and for me, I can choose my own shampoo, makeup, soap, makeup remover etc.

I always try to go for package-free, chemical-free products if possible. My number-one swap would be bamboo toothbrushes and toothpaste tablets. My face wash and my face moisturizer containers are reusable and refillable. It is also vegan, cruelty free, biodegradable, palm-oil free and yes, zero waste from Plaine Products, which by the way is a carbon-neutral company.

Unfortunately, there is no such thing as 100% zero waste nail polish, but there is low waste and more importantly, chemical-free nail polish and removers. You want to avoid glitter nail polish because glitter in nail polish is essentially microplastics that don't break down and end up in our oceans.

My favorite brands

Nails For nail polish I like the brands Kapanui Nails, Habit Cosmetics, and Karma Organic. And for nail polish remover I use Karma organic soybean oil nail polish remover.

Formal wear Let me tell you something. From experience, you will not wear your formal wear again. It will sit in your childhood closet until you donate it. Since most guys rent tuxes for formal events, we should take a cue from them and give renting a try.

There are TONS of websites like Rent the Runway, Join Wardrobe, and even Macy's that will let you rent gorgeous designer dresses for a fraction of the price of owning a dress. They have so many options, and you'll save valuable closet space.

Be a minimal and thrifty Fashionista

"Hello, I'm Isabella and I'm a minimal fashionista who loves second hand clothes." The majority of my clothes – except underwear, swimwear and socks – are secondhand and fabulous. I feel so lucky to grow up in a time when thrift shopping is considered a "thing," and all over social media, fashion influencers share their thrift shop outfits, thrift shopping has become cool. The best part about second hand fashion is that it's rare to run into someone wearing the same outfit. I always give my clothes that I have outgrown to friends who are smaller and younger than me. Old t-shirts that have stains or holes become rags for cleaning and extra fabrics for craft projects.

For the clothes I do not buy second hand, I like to make sure they are organic and high quality. Compared to my friends, I do not own as many clothes, so my closet is quite minimal, and people are so surprised to hear I only own 4 pairs of shoes: tennis shoes, boots, sandals ,and converse, and two pairs of pants, which are both jeans. The fact is that I only need that many; and this way, my room and closet is always clean and organized.

Get Involved

See if there's a local organization you can get plugged into around your town or school. Volunteer for a beach cleanup or pick up trash around town. Get involved!

Make protecting the environment, picking up trash, or fighting climate change one of your extracurricular activities. Not only will it look good on that college resume, but your parents are more likely to get involved, too, just by association.

Be fashionable in second-hand finds or choose fewer clothes, but make sure they are sustainable and high quality to make them last.

I have so far been volunteering cleaning beaches with Surf Riders, worked with Produce Goods to reduce food waste, and protested with SanDiego350.org and Oceana. Bring your friends and get involved. Turning worries about climate change into action is my motto.

Take responsibility

Take the initiative and help out cooking dinner, grocery shopping, and cleaning and helping make the eco-friendly decisions.

This can be an opportunity to take control of one aspect, then you can try it out with zero waste. And if it works, it might inspire your family to give it a try! Remember to take small steps, one at the time. Start by swapping out one disposable item for a reusable — one at the time.

Talk to your parents

The most important thing you can do is educate your family and friends; however, make sure not to preach. Nagging won't get you anywhere. But, when you're truly interested and excited about something, you want to share it.

Maybe suggest a documentary on trash like *The True Cost* or *The Minimalists* or *The Clean Bin Project,* on movie night. This might open the door for a conversation about climate change and waste. Tell your parents you would like to learn about climate change together, and tell them how you feel about climate change.

Try a mother-daughter date

My mom and I have fun trying new recipes for making our own makeup remover, face mask, lip balm, crafts, or anything that is waste free and a fun activity to do with my family.

Chapter 21
Zero Waste Traveling

"You cannot get through a single day without having an impact on the world around you. What you do makes a difference, and you have to decide what kind of difference you want to make."

— Jane Goodall,
Global community conservationist

Living a zero waste lifestyle can be challenging enough when you are surrounded by the comforts of home — so how can it be doable when you step out of your comfort zone? Traveling undoubtedly poses more of a challenge.

My family travels to Sweden every summer, as that's where I was raised. Sure, the very best zero waste option would be to never travel by flying — but for most, this is just simply unrealistic. Instead, we must do the very best we can to reduce our impact while we travel.

If you care about the environment but also need to travel, here's a list of ideas my family follows for reducing our carbon footprint:

1. Buy a carbon offset program from the airline

Many airlines today offer carbon offset programs, which are carbon calculators designed to alleviate the impact of greenhouse gas emissions from fossil fuels by making tax-deductible charitable contributions to a variety of independently reviewed and certified environmental projects focused on forest conservation, renewable energy, and preventing deforestation. After booking your flight, you're given the option to calculate your emissions and offset your carbon, or you can just visit the airline's carbon offset website. Then you'll enter either your itinerary information or the dollar amount that you'd like to contribute.

Fact!

Over six tons of airplane cabin waste is created every year! With some smart planning you can do your part to reduce that.

Most packed meals on planes are not good and come with lots of plastic, so we always pack our own food in bento boxes and bring them when we travel.

2. Refuse a meal on the plane and bring your own

Most of the meals on flights are packaged in lots of plastic. In my opinion, they are not even that good — so the greener option is to give the flight attendants the heads up that you will be opting out of your meal and bringing your own food instead. I personally love packing homemade food for our family in plastic-free bento boxes from Lunchbot or from ReVessel.com.

When traveling, we always bring an array of snacks and treat for kids. This way we avoid overspending on single-packaged foods.

Here's the food we often bring when Traveling

- Homemade raw granola with berries (in a mason jar)
- Nuts
- Crackers
- Avocado
- Salad or sandwiches

- Cold noodle salad
- Quinoa salad
- Hummus
- Raw veggies and crackers to dip

Our family always brings our own reusable water bottles, napkins and cutleries when traveling anywhere, so we can reduce as much waste as possible even during our trip.

3. Supply your own water bottle

Almost all airports these days have water bottle refill stations. This is an easy way to fill up your water bottles before your flight to avoid plastic cups onboard.

In order to reduce as much as possible when traveling, we always bring reusable coffee cups , water bottles, and each family member's own reusable cutlery set.

4. Bring your own coffee cup, napkins, and cutlery

We always bring a reusable coffee cup and get our java to-go before flying. Sometimes, if you ask nicely, flight attendants will even give you coffee in them. A cloth napkin is light and easy to bring and can be used instead of paper napkins. Skip the plastic cutlery and bring your own reusable option.

We like to stay in a home instead of hotels when we travel, so we can cook our own food. We pack reusable bags for shopping in local grocery stores and farmers markets.

5. Bring cloth shopping bags

Not only are they great for carrying groceries, stocking up on bulk food at the farmers market or grocery stores — they're also perfect for the beach.

6. Pack lightly

The less stuff you bring with you, the smaller your carbon footprint will be. Just think about the cost of transporting your luggage and the resources necessary to wash and iron your clothes while traveling. Even if your child is still a baby, be practical about the essentials. For example, there are various eco-friendly luggage bags available that can make your packing a lot easier.

It's a fact that most people pack too much, and there is nothing more annoying than lugging around too many heavy suitcases when traveling — especially for a family of five! We usually pack enough clothes for one week and try to pack clothes that can be mixed and matched. Also, think layers for cooler days and nights. For longer trips, I always bring soap nuts so I can wash clothes throughout the trip.

A mason jar with lid is a great item to travel with. It can be used for compost to add your food scraps, something to bring a snack in, or a glass for a drink.

7. Become best friends with Mason jars

Mason jars with lids are amazing and can be used for so much: as a wine glass on a plane or train, for iced coffee at coffee shops, as food storage, or even a compost container to keep your food scraps in until you reach a compost bin!

8. Use electronic tickets for flights, transportation, events, etc.

9. Bring your own headphones for inflight entertainment

10. Don't buy new magazines, books, or newspapers for travel

Instead, borrow books from the library, buy used magazines, or download books onto your phone or tablet. Also, skip the newspapers if offered on flights.

11. Stay in Airbnbs or apartments

HomeExchange.com is also a great option for swapping homes with another family. This is how we like to travel because we can cook our own food and prepare snacks to take with us when we're out. This saves money and lots of waste from eating at restaurants. Usually, these homes come with a washing machine so you can do your own laundry, too. To stay green while doing laundry, I always bring soap nuts. Bonus: our kids generally feel a bit more relaxed in a home rather than in a hotel because they have more space to move around and play.

12. Supply your own zero waste shampoo, soap, and lotion

Biking is a great way to get around, tour a new city, and get some exercise at the same time. Most cities have bike rentals available and might even offer bike tours.

13. Bring activated charcoal for water filters

Instead of buying bottled water, we bring activated charcoal for filtering water. It's inexpensive and light to pack.

14. Use public transportation, bike, or walk whenever possible

If the place where you're staying has public transportation, be sure to use it instead of renting a car or taking a taxi to get around. Moreover, if the place is fairly small, maximize the opportunity to go on meaningful walks with your kids. And, even better — exploring on a bike doubles the fun while significantly minimizing your carbon footprint. In my opinion, there is no more exciting way to see a city than walking or biking through it. These days, most cities have easy-access bikes for rent.

15. Prioritize experiences over material goods

Before your trip, make sure to have a purposeful and engaging conversation with your kids explaining that traveling is ultimately about the bonding that happens with shared experiences rather than shopping for things. Taking the time to encourage your kids to value the experience of travel more than anything else not only will help you stay green on your vacations, but will also make your children's lives more fulfilling.

16. Decline daily fresh towels and sheets (if staying in a hotel)

17. Return plastic room keys to the front desk (if staying in a hotel)

18. Say "no" to disposable items

    Usually on flights and in hotels, you tend to receive a lot of small, individually packaged items like warm towels, plastic-wrapped blankets, snacks, toothbrushes, and shampoos. Most of them are either made of or packed in plastic, so I have a habit of saying "no" to all disposable goods.

19. Find a local farmers market or organic grocery store in your location

    I just absolutely love visiting farmers markets in different cities and countries — and eating local foods is such a fun experience.

Most importantly, don't let your zero waste lifestyle take away from enjoying your trip — life's way too short for that.

Bon Voyage!

Chapter 22

Zero Waste on a Budget

"Why try to explain miracles to your kids when
you can just have them plant a garden."

– Robert Brault

There's an assumption that living a zero waste lifestyle has to be expensive, and that you need to buy a bunch of zero waste products to get started. It's true that you will have to replace some disposable products with reusable ones, but it sure doesn't have to be expensive. Zero waste actually saves you money in the long run, and there are many ways to get started — even on a budget.

Tips for Zero Waste on a Budget:

1. **Use glass jars with lids — and they don't have to be new.**

   I have said this before and I will say it again — jars are essential to living a zero waste lifestyle. But you do not have to go out and buy brand new ones. Look at thrift markets or ask around. Lots of people are happy to part with their mason jars.

2. **Use what you have before replacing with zero waste.**

   Once you have made the decision to reduce waste, don't throw out all your unsustainable products to replace them with zero waste, reusable products. That is not sustainable — so first use up what you have, and then replace as you run out.

3. **Make your own grocery and produce bags.**

   Buy inexpensive pillowcases at a thrift shop and make them into reusable grocery and produce bags. AWasteNotKindofLife.com has tutorials on how to make produce bags and LifeIsMade.com has videos on making grocery bags.

4. **Make your own cloth paper towels.**

   All you need are scraps of fabric or an old towel to make some.

5. **Make your own household cleaners.**

   To clean things around your home, you probably go through many different cleaning solutions. Commercial cleaning ingredients include harsh chemicals that aren't good for the environment after they get washed down the drain. Plus, buying a large jug of dishwasher or laundry detergent can be pretty expensive. Instead, you can make your own solution by combining one-part water to one-part white vinegar. Add a few lemon rinds to increase the acidity and some baking soda for tough cleaning spots like the grout between your shower tiles. One 64 oz bottle of distilled vinegar costs $2.64 and one pound of baking soda costs $0.82 at Walmart (and that will last you a long time).

6. **Make a meal plan and stick to it.**

   Meal planning has saved my sanity and my budget. I have found that with just a little smart planning and food prep, weekday dinners are a breeze. Because I plan ahead, we also have reduced food waste — which also saves money.

7. **Go meat-free.**

   Meat can cost a lot at the grocery store, often averaging $4 per pound or more. If you're cooking to feed a family, that's multiple pounds of meat with each meal. Skip meat once a week and enjoy a vegetarian dish instead. You can buy two pounds of pinto beans for $1.29. You'll save money and give the meat industry fewer reasons to devour resources.

How to Eat Organic and Sustainably on a Budget

Eating healthfully on a budget might seem like an impossible task — especially with children. Believe me, I get it. I'm raising three hungry children while also focusing on organic and healthy, plant-based food. A few years ago, our food bill was too high. Over the past few years, I've adopted a few tricks that help us eat organic and healthy on less money. These days, our food bill is about $700 per month to feed five people eating only organic food — and that includes packed school lunches (and we parents eat lunch at home everyday).

Here's how we do it

1. **We shop at our local farmers market once a week.**

   Then every two weeks we grocery shop at our co-op for all our staple foods like milk, yogurt, butter, oats, pasta, rice, beans, etc.

2. **We make a budget and stick to it.**

   I have given our family a budget of $800 per month, which includes eating out occasionally. I truly believe that setting a firm budget is a huge help because it means I buy only what we need, and it pushes me to intentionally search for the best deals.

3. **We skip pre-packaged foods and go for bulk instead.**

   Pre-packaged food might be convenient, but it's usually more expensive, and it's not very good for the planet. At our local co-op, I buy lots of snacks in bulk, which saves me money and reduces waste. I don't buy very many canned foods and, being vegetarian, beans are the staple in our diet. I cook dried beans in large quantities in a crockpot, then freeze smaller portions in recycled glass jars. On Sundays, I bake all our bread for the week and then freeze it.

4. **Reduce food waste.**

   Half of all waste in landfills is food waste because we have a tendency to waste food and to forget about what is in our fridge or freezer. Before our budget changed, we would throw away food that had spoiled by the end of the week. If we ran out of something — well, we simply went to the store and bought more. Nowadays, I make meals from the food we have available at home, strategically using fresh food first. At the end of the week, I use the vegetables that are getting soft or limp for stir-fries and soups.

Other tips for reducing food cost

1. **Sign up for a CSA box.**

   Community Supported Agriculture (CSA) boxes usually are packed with local, seasonal, and organic produce — and usually at an affordable price.

2. **Look out for sales.**

   When our local grocery store had a sale on organic bananas, we loaded up and froze a ton for smoothies, ice cream, and banana bread. Lots of markets offer discounted food products, so be sure not to miss out.

3. **Buy in bulk.**

   Bulk foods like grains, flour, nuts, seeds, beans, lentils, and granola are usually cheaper than packaged foods—so load up!

Eating homegrown food or food that is 'in season' saves not only the planet, since food does not have to travel so far, but it also saves money.

4. Eat in season.

We eat local food as much as possible, and we eat for the season — meaning that during winter, our fruits are mostly oranges and apples. Before, we used to eat kiwi and strawberries (and anything else we fancied) even though they weren't "winter foods." Now, those are treats when they appear at the farmers market during summer months.

5. Grow food.

Needless to say, growing your own food saves money, is good for the planet, and is zero waste. Even if you don't have a large garden and just have a patio, you can still grow food! Whether in my garden or on my patio, I've always grown food like kale, tomatoes, lettuce, sprouts, and potatoes—just to name a few.

To sum it up, here's how we lowered our food bill

- Buy local as much as possible.
- Eat for the season.
- Grocery shop only once per week – and stick to it!
- Limit buying canned goods.
- Buy in bulk as much as possible — it's better for the environment and your wallet.
- Have at least one meat-free day per week — meat and fish are expensive.
- Serve lots of fruits and vegetables with each meal — they are better for your health and will fill your tummies too.
- Be creative at the end of the week and use what you have at home — leftover vegetables and beans can become wonderful soups, pasta dishes, stir-fries, and stews.
- Use leftovers the next day to cook another meal — leftover pasta can be a fun pasta salad, leftover chicken can be used for sandwiches, etc.
- Clean out your fridge and freezer often to take inventory of what you have, and then build a meal plan from that. So many times I have found food that would have been wasted otherwise!
- Grow your own food.

Chapter 23

Zero Waste and the Financial Benefits

"We can't just consume our way to a more sustainable world."

– Jennifer Nini

Many people ask me exactly how we save money with zero waste. I knew that going zero waste would save the planet — but saving money in the process was a pleasant surprise. I say it's the fun bonus of our efforts. We finally did some calculations on how much we've saved annually since going zero waste, and the amount is a whopping $18,000 per year.

Here are our tips for saving money while saving the planet

1. **Reduce food waste.**

   According to a report by the Natural Resources Defense Council's (NRDC) food and agriculture program, the average American family throws away 40 percent of their food, which adds up to $2,275 annually. I have to admit that we used to throw out food, too; however, these days I try to use everything by freezing leftovers like cheese, onions, etc. I even make breadcrumbs from end pieces of bread or stale bread, and make soups and stews from the veggies about to go downhill. At the end of the week, I take inventory of what we have left and write it down so I can see what we have and then make dishes from it. Today, we waste very little food and save lots of money in the process.

2. **Replace disposable items with reusable ones.**

   By investing in reusable items, you will save lots of money. Yes, naturally, there is the initial cost — but depending on how much you buy and for how long you use it,

We always bring our own reusable bottles for water, coffee, or tea since store bought is way more expensive and comes with more waste.

you can save quite a bit. For example, we used cloth diapers and wipes for our kids. It's no secret that diapers (both cloth and disposable) are expensive. But the benefit of cloth diapers is that they are a one-time expense, and the diapers should last throughout the child's diapers years (and then perhaps also be used for a sibling). I used my cloth diapers for each of my kids and at one point, for both my boys simultaneously. So I used my cloth diapers for six years in total. If you then count the cost of a package of diapers (let's say once a month for a large package of diapers from Target at the cost of $39, not including tax), that saves about $2,800 — which does not include switching from disposable wipes to reusable ones. Cloth diapers also have a good resale value, so once we were finished with diapers, I sold them and got at least half my money back. In addition to switching to cloth diapers, we've also saved money by skipping paper plates, cups, party cutlery, paper towels, plastic food wrap, zip lock bags, disposable water bottles, and more.

3. Pack lunches.

We pack lunches every day for our kids and ourselves, and we do it without any waste by skipping snacks and foods that come in disposable packaging. Instead, we eat leftovers from the previous day's dinner or make sandwiches, salads, wraps, and snacks from the bulk section. Lunch can cost $4 for something like a cup of soup and a roll or even $15 (at least) for a full sit-down lunch in a restaurant. So,

Bring food and have a picnic when going anywhere with the kids. Food tastes better when eaten outdoors anyway.

let's say an average daily lunch costs about $10 while a homemade lunch could bring the cost down to approximately $2-$5. That's a total of $160 savings per month for five lunches a week!

4. Ride your bike more often.

Instead of using the car, save money by biking, walking, or taking public transportation to your destinations. According to AAA, owning and driving a car costs about $8,500 a year; whereas owning and operating a bike costs $350. So, if it is possible to commute by bike, this will save money. My family bikes as much as possible. We used to have baby seats and a trailer to bring the younger kids along, and now that the kids are older they all ride their own bikes. It's great because the kids love the bike ride, we save the environment and money, and we get exercise at the same time. If public transportation is not possible for you, and you have to take the car, try combining errands into a single trip or carpooling with others..

5. Buy used whenever possible.

At one time, buying used goods was associated with those who couldn't afford to shop for new. Today, it's the trendy and environmentally conscious thing to do. Many fashionable, eco-conscious social media stars shop secondhand to keep

Bike or walk instead of taking the car everywhere.

clothes out of landfills as much as to keep money in their pockets. Clothes are not the only thing that can be shopped secondhand— toys, books, china, and much more can be found for little money (and with a smaller carbon footprint).

6. Repair — don't dispose.

I don't have to explain how repairing broken items instead of throwing them out and buying new will save money. Let's face it, repairing something is not difficult, and these days you can google how to fix pretty much anything. If your garment is missing a button, learn how to sew it back on. If a zipper is broken, learn how to fix it. If there is a small hole or stain, learn how to cover it the fashionable way.

7. Make homemade cleaning products.

Though there are many recipes for making your own cleaning solutions, the basic ingredients are distilled vinegar and baking soda. With the right recipes, you could come up with highly effective solutions. In fact, most DIY cleaners cost less than $1 while most store-bought products cost about $3-$15. Such figures beg the question: Why would you want to spend more on harmful products when you could spend less, stay safe, and produce less waste?

Learn the basic skills of mending holes and buttons, and you can save many clothes.

8. Make coffee instead of buying.

I know there are days when a strong cup of coffee is the only thing that's keeping you going, but try getting your caffeine fix at home rather than at the coffee shop. It might not seem like a lot of money for that cup, but since one latte can cost about $5, just multiply that by seven and see how much it costs in one week. By making coffee at home and having a reusable coffee mug to take on the go, you will save around $140 per month. If you're not ready to give up Starbucks, then choose regular coffee because it's cheaper. And bring your own reusable cup since lots of coffee places will give a discount for that.

9. Buy organic food at your local farmers market.

It's local, which means less carbon dioxide — and it's cheaper. If you don't have access to a farmers market, subscribe to a CSA box from a local farm.

10. Wash clothes in cold water.

Modern-day detergents don't need hot water to work, and since 90% of the energy used for washing clothes is used to heat the water— you really can cut costs and go green by washing in cold water. Furthermore, since hot water tends to bleach colors, washing in cold water will also save your brightly colored clothes.

Skip going to a coffee shop and brew your own coffee and tea for a lot less money.

11. Use soap nuts.

My family has been washing our clothes and cloth diapers with soap nuts for years — we love them. A one pound bag costs about $20, and lasts forever. You use about five soap nuts in a small bag with each load, and you can wash about 3–5 loads of laundry with the same nuts. They're biodegradable, so afterward you can throw them onto the compost.

12. Hang-dry laundry.

Hang-drying laundry is a little more work, but it saves so much energy (and saves your clothes, too). We invested in an Ikea drying rack that can be folded and stored when we're not using it.

13. Grow your own food.

Even if you're not blessed with a garden where you can grow your own food, there are many things you can grow on a balcony or even indoors. Sprouts are an easy, chlorophyll-rich vegetable to grow indoors. Tomatoes, potatoes, and lettuce can be grown in buckets and pots on a balcony.

14. Use recycled items for kids crafts.

Save print paper, old cardboard boxes, old toilet paper rolls, newspaper and textiles to use for kids' crafts. It's amazing what you can do with all this stuff. We have made a Barbie house and clothes, bird feeders and pirate hats from lots of recycled stuff. Our kids will look at a box and ask, "So, what can we do with this?"

15. Use cloth diapers and wipes.

Cloth diapers and wipes might be expensive, but they're a one-time purchase. It will reduce trash that stays in the landfill for 100 years and save you money in the long run because the cost of diapers and wipes for about 2 years per child is pricey.

16. Do free online and/or workouts outside.

The best thing I ever did was to skip my gym, paid for online classes, and headed outside for my workout. These days, I hike, bike, power walk or run for exercise; and it's completely free.

As you can see, by not going green, you're flushing money down the drain. Paying attention and making small changes will help you save money that could be used for more fun things. Saving money while minimizing your family's carbon footprint is a win-win situation in my mind.

Small Steps Make a Big Impact

Fact!

The average American family throws away 40 percent of their food, which adds up to $2,275 annually.

Source Natural Resources Defense Council

Chapter 24

Zero Waste Film

Zero Time To Waste documentary is a compelling, hopeful portrait of a family striving to be conscious citizens in a consumer culture.

The film *Zero Time to Waste* follows our family's journey of living zero waste in the middle of San Diego — a social movement we hope to see grow as we work to inspire small changes in our local community. By growing our own food, not producing any waste, choosing alternative transportation, and saving $18,000 annually in the process, everyday tasks are more intentional, and we're happier for it.

This compelling portrait is a hopeful reimagining of what it looks like to be conscious citizens in the midst of daunting statistics and the peak of consumer culture. Combining social theory, environmental research, and a heartwarming glimpse into one family's path, this film encapsulates the idea of being the change you wish to see as there really is no time to waste.

You can find out how to watch the film at ZeroTimeToWaste.com

Conclusion

"We don't have to engage in grand, heroic actions to participate in change.
Small acts, when multiplied by millions of people, can transform the world."

– Howard Zinn,
Historian, playwright, and activist

I hope this guide will help begin your own journey to reducing waste. I recommend starting slowly and one step at the time. Find one disposable item you use and find a waste-free option for it. And when you're ready, find the next one. This is the most sustainable and doable way to reduce your carbon footprint. Good luck, and enjoy this journey, and be kind to yourself in this process.

Zero Waste Family Resource List

"The strongest governments on earth cannot clean up pollution by themselves. They must rely on each ordinary person, like you and me, on our choices, and on our will."

– Chai Jing,
Chinese journalist, author and environmental activist

Zero Waste Lifestyle Brands

Life without plastic | Lifewithoutplastic.com

Plastic Free Pursuit| plasticfreepursuit.com

Eco Roots | ecoroots.us

Package Free Shop | packagefreeshop.com

Mindful Goods | mindfulgoods.com

The Waste Less Shop | thewastelessshop.com!

A Public Shop | apublicshop.com

Goldrick Natural Living | goldricknaturalliving.com.

No Tox Life | notoxlife.com.

Scoop Marketplace | scoopmarketplace.com

Protea | proteazerowaste.com

Zerovana | zerovana.com.

Wild Minimalist | wildminimalist.com

Tare Market | thetaremarket.com

Good Intent | shopwithgoodintent.com

The zero-waste store| https://zerowastestore.com

Sustainability Influencers

Ryan | My Niagara Garden
Rob Greenfield
Sustainable Kikki
Rainbow Vegan Rocks
Anisa/ Circular Lifestyle
My_ journey _to_ zerowaste
Sustainable Shelby
The Fairly Local Family

Kids Brands

Hanna Andersson |Hannaandersson.com
Pact| Wearpact.com
Mini Mate|Matethelable.com
Primary| Primary.com
Jackalo| Hellojackalo.com
Colored Organics|Coloredorganics.com
Petit Tembo|Petittembo.com
Borobabi|Borobabi.com

Cloth Diapers

Esembly Baby|Esemblybaby.com
Bumgenius|Bumgenius.com
Green Mountain diapers|https://www.greenmountaindiapers.com
Nickis diapers|Nickidiapers.com

Zero Waste Toys

Earth Hero |https://earthhero.com/product-category/baby-kids/toys/
Begin Again Toys| https://www.beginagaintoys.com
Lie Wood Toys|https://www.liewood.com/collections/indoor-toys
PlanToys |Plantoys.com
Le Toy Van|Letoyvan.com
HABA |Habausa.com
Tender Leaf Toys| Tenderleaftoys.com
Hape | Hapetoys.com
Maple Landmark|Maplelandmark.com
Tegu|Tegu.com

Sustainable Fashion Brands Women

Prana|Prana.com
Pantagonia|Pantagonia.com
Lululemon|Lululemon.com

Sustainable Fashion Brands Men

Unbound|Unbound.com
Bluffworks|Bluffworks.com
Pantagonia|Pantagonia.com

Swimwear

Aqua Green |Aquagreen.net

Kitchen + On The Go Dining

Life without Plastic | Lifewithoutplastic.com
Package Free Shop | packagefreeshop.com/collections/on-the-go
Net Zero Company | www.netzerocompany.com

Acknowledgements

I want to thank Kim Robson. Some sections of this book are inspired from articles she wrote with me at my former site Green-Mom.com over the past 8 years.

Photography Jamie Street (jamiestreet.com), Julia Larson Saperstein (jlsfoto.com) and Elena Shur (elenashurphotography.com)

Additional Photography Zlatko Duric, Laura Ohlman, Lisa Woakes, Maria Shanina, Alexander Mils, Damir Spanic

Editing Rebekah Pahl and Sheryn Wright. Second Edition, BBL Publishing.

Illustrations Harrison Weather

Publisher Leann Garms, BBL Publishing
An imprint of Build.Buzz.Launch. Media & Publishing

Public Relations Kimberly King Media, Kimberly King and Shanna Schwarz

Administrative Assistant Maddie Mackey

Merave Segall, LMFT, Advice on talking to children about climate change

Join the movement at www.ZeroWasteFamily.com

Index

Fredrika Syren, Author and activist

About
The Author

Fredrika Syren is an environmental activist and writer who has a passion for gardening and cooking. In 2011, she founded the website green-mom.com where she shared her family's journey of living zero waste. She lives in San Diego, California, on an urban homestead with her husband, James, and their children Isabella, Noah, and Liam. Fredrika and her family have been interviewed across many TV networks like *CBS*, *FOX*, *Nickelodeon*, *WGN*, *ABC*, *The Dr. Oz Show,* in the documentary *Zero Time to Waste,* and American filmmaker Ava DuVernay's TV series *"Home Sweet Home"* on *NBC*.